The Essence of the Christian Faith

The Essence of the Christian Faith

A 1689 Confession for the 21st Century

ADAM MURRELL

RESOURCE *Publications* · Eugene, Oregon

THE ESSENCE OF THE CHRISTIAN FAITH
A 1689 Confession for the 21st Century

Resource Publications
A Division of Wipf and Stock Publishers
199 W. 8th Ave., Suite 3
Eugene, OR 97401
www.wipfandstock.com

ISBN13: 978-1-49825-310-9

With deep gratitude to the ministers and messengers in England and Wales who met together in London in 1689 to consider some things that might be for the glory of God and the good of congregations in order to adopt a confession of faith.

Contents

Note to the Reader

My oldest daughter discovered a love for picnics shortly before her second birthday. Every occasion to eat renewed the possibility of picnicking outside in the Mississippi Gulf Coast breeze while under the outstretched branches of the southern magnolias, on the front porch rocker, or beneath the patio umbrella. We could eat just about anywhere—other than the dinner table—and it was a picnic to her. The times we indulged her requests, her glimmering eyes would sparkle with excitement as she waited anxiously to be served. It was of little concern to her whether the food was nutritious or if it varied in flavor. Only a select few items would satisfy her appetite, none of which could be classified as constituting a well-balanced meal.

Many professing Christians today have a spiritual diet reminiscent of my daughter's desired meals, in that they do not care about variety, flavor, or quality of spiritual food—they just want what tastes pleasing. Peter declared that we should be like newborn infants, longing for the spiritual milk that will help us to grow (1 Pet 2:2). That is to say, we should desire the purity of God's Word so that we will be nourished.

If I surrendered to my daughter's inclination to eat only what she wanted then her growth would be hindered severely. Similarly, we will stunt our spiritual growth if we do not feed our appetites with thorough biblical study. A good appetite that enjoys a well-balanced meal is one sign of good health. If a believer does not have an appetite for the whole counsel of God, then he becomes emaciated and his soul goes unnourished—or at least undernourished. The only antidote to malnutrition is to eat regularly and in a healthy manner.

This little book is an appetizer for the spiritually hungry. It contains meat from the *Baptist Confession of Faith of 1689* that has been the standard confession in many Baptist churches worldwide for more than three centuries. The *1689* has been honored, respected, and used by some of the greatest theologians, including Charles Spurgeon who called the confession "the best expression of the Christian faith." I concur. I believe the *1689* is the "best expression," because it is the repository of Christian orthodoxy regarding the Bible, the Trinity, the Person of Christ, and the sovereignty of God. Spurgeon recognized the need for Christians to have a concise summation of the historic faith that was delivered once to the saints (Jude 1:3). He also realized the *1689* was a treasure of truth that could help believers progress in their Christian maturation.

I invite you to come with me on a spiritual picnic. Find a relaxing atmosphere and enjoy some spiritual nourishment by delving into God's Word as expressed through this historic confession of faith that has lasted through the centuries. It will be sure to satisfy your hunger.

Adam Murrell
King George, Virginia

The Holy Bible

Question 1–1: What is the Holy Bible?

Answer: The Holy Bible is the only certain and infallible rule of all saving knowledge, faith, and obedience that constitute salvation. *(a) (b) (c) (d)*

(a) But Abraham said, "They have Moses and the Prophets; let them hear them" (Luke 16:29).

(b) He said to him, "If they do not hear Moses and the Prophets, neither will they be convinced if someone should rise from the dead" (Luke 16:31).

(c) Built on the foundation of the apostles and prophets, Christ Jesus himself being the cornerstone (Eph 2:20).

(d) And how from childhood you have been acquainted with the sacred writings, which are able to make you wise for salvation through faith in Christ Jesus. All Scripture is breathed out by God and profitable for teaching, for reproof, for correction, and for training in righteousness, that the man of God may be competent, equipped for every good work (2 Tim 3:15–17).

Remarks: The Bible is certain and infallible because it is from God. It is through the 66 books of Holy Scripture that he has chosen to make himself known. No one would have an understanding of who God was had he not first acted to relate himself in a personal manner. The Bible was chosen as the means by which to reveal his will about what we are to believe for salvation and the duties he requires of his creation.

QUESTION 1–2: WHAT ARE THE 66 BOOKS OF THE BIBLE?

ANSWER: The Old Testament consists of 39 books: Genesis, Exodus, Leviticus, Numbers, Deuteronomy, Joshua, Judges, Ruth, 1–2 Samuel, 1–2 Kings, 1–2 Chronicles, Ezra, Nehemiah, Esther, Job, Psalms, Proverbs, Ecclesiastes, The Song of Solomon, Isaiah, Jeremiah, Lamentations, Ezekiel, Daniel, Hosea, Joel, Amos, Obadiah, Jonah, Micah, Nahum, Habakkuk, Zephaniah, Haggai, Zechariah, Malachi.

The New Testament consists of 27 books: Matthew, Mark, Luke, John, The Acts of the Apostles, Paul's Epistle to the Romans, 1–2 Corinthians, Galatians, Ephesians, Philippians, Colossians, 1–2 Thessalonians, 1–2 Timothy, Titus, Philemon, The Epistle to the Hebrews, Epistle of James, 1–2 Peter, 1–2–3 John, Jude, and Revelation.

Each book of the Bible is given by the inspiration of God to be the rule of faith and life. *(a)*

> *(a)* All Scripture is breathed out by God and profitable for teaching, for reproof, for correction, and for training in righteousness (2 Tim 3:16).

REMARKS: The Bible is a book. It might also be called a collection of books compiled together into one volume. We call the book the "Holy Bible" because it is directly from God. The 66 books contained in the Bible were written over the course of 1,600 years with at least 40 different authors. The Old Testament was written primarily in Hebrew—with some Aramaic—while the New Testament was penned in the common Greek. Despite the vast diversity of authorship and the length of time it took to complete the canon, we have one continuous and harmonious book that is first among all others. The Holy Bible is the measuring rod by which all norms are to be judged.

QUESTION 1–3: WHAT IS THE APOCRYPHA?

ANSWER: The books commonly called the Apocrypha are the extra-biblical writings that are not divinely inspired and are not part of the canon of Scripture. These books are of no authority in the church of God. *(a) (b) (c)*

> *(a)* And beginning with Moses and all the Prophets, he interpreted to them in all the Scriptures the things concerning himself (Luke 24:27).

(b) Then he said to them, "These are my words that I spoke to you while I was still with you, that everything written about me in the Law of Moses and the Prophets and the Psalms must be fulfilled" (Luke 24:44).

(c) Much in every way. To begin with, the Jews were entrusted with the oracles of God (Rom 3:2).

REMARKS: Apocryphal means "hidden" or "of doubtful authenticity." The Apocrypha refers to the collection of books written during the Intertestamental Period, the four centuries separating the book of Malachi and the first chapter of the New Testament. By the time of Jesus Christ, the Hebrew canon was established but did not include the apocryphal writings. This is important because Paul reveals to us that the Jews were entrusted with the oracles of God (Rom 3:2). The Apocrypha was not accepted as canonical until the Council of Trent in the sixteenth century officially and authoritatively established it for the Roman Catholic Church.

QUESTION 1–4: WHAT IS THE BASIS FOR BELIEVING THE SCRIPTURES TO BE AUTHORITATIVE?

ANSWER: The Bible is authoritative because God is the author. *(a) (b)*

(a) All Scripture is breathed out by God and profitable for teaching, for reproof, for correction, and for training in righteousness (2 Tim 3:16).

(b) If we receive the testimony of men, the testimony of God is greater, for this is the testimony of God that he has borne concerning his Son (1 John 5:9).

REMARKS: The central argument for the authority of the Bible is the testimony of Jesus Christ. He affirmed the Old Testament Scriptures as the "God–breathed" revelation from his Father (Matt 5:17–20, 26:52–54; Luke 10:25–26, 16:17). By virtue of being a revelation from God, the Bible is given preeminence among all other authorities. Unlike oral traditions outside of Scripture, the written words of God are not subject to change, deviation, or corruption.

QUESTION 1–5: HOW DO WE UNDERSTAND THE BIBLE'S MESSAGE?

ANSWER: The Holy Spirit infallibly communicates truth to us and through the testimony of the church of God, as she is faithful to the Word. *(a) (b) (c) (d)*

> *(a)* When the Spirit of truth comes, he will guide you into all the truth, for he will not speak on his own authority, but whatever he hears he will speak, and he will declare to you the things that are to come. He will glorify me, for he will take what is mine and declare it to you (John 16:13–14).

> *(b)* These things God has revealed to us through the Spirit. For the Spirit searches everything, even the depths of God. For who knows a person's thoughts except the spirit of that person, which is in him? So also no one comprehends the thoughts of God except the Spirit of God. Now we have received not the spirit of the world, but the Spirit who is from God, that we might understand the things freely given us by God (1 Cor 2:10–12).

> *(c)* But you have been anointed by the Holy One, and you all have knowledge (1 John 2:20).

> *(d)* But the anointing that you received from him abides in you, and you have no need that anyone should teach you. But as his anointing teaches you about everything, and is true, and is no lie—just as it has taught you, abide in him (1 John 2:27).

REMARKS: The Holy Spirit has come to convey the truths to us that Jesus once taught. This is not to say, however, that the Holy Spirit comes to grant temporal knowledge of every kind. Instead, the Spirit delivers the truth about God, just as he did when he inspired the writing of Scripture.

QUESTION 1–6: WHAT ASPECTS OF MAN'S LIFE DOES THE BIBLE COVER?

ANSWER: The Bible covers all things necessary concerning God's glory, man's salvation, and faith and life. *(a) (b)*

> *(a)* But even if we or an angel from heaven should preach to you a gospel contrary to the one we preached to you, let him be ac-

cursed. As we have said before, so now I say again: If anyone is preaching to you a gospel contrary to the one you received let him be accursed (Gal 1:8–9).

(b) And how from childhood you have been acquainted with the sacred writings, which are able to make you wise for salvation through faith in Christ Jesus. All Scripture is breathed out by God and profitable for teaching, for reproof, for correction, and for training in righteousness, that the man of God may be competent, equipped for every good work (2 Tim 3:15–17).

REMARKS: The Bible is God's written Word through which he imposes his absolute obligation upon his creation. It expresses the nature of mankind after the fall of man and outlines the pathway of redemption. Every Christian is called to have a mature understanding of what that entails but can only come to this knowledge through a diligent study of God's Word. If we meditate upon Scripture continually, the Lord will grant us truth that we might know how to live our lives in a manner that is pleasing unto him.

QUESTION 1–7: WHO CAN UNDERSTAND THE WAY OF SALVA-
TION AS EXPRESSED IN THE BIBLE?

ANSWER: All things in the Bible are not plainly alike nor are they clear to all people. (a) Yet, everything that is necessary to be known and believed for salvation is so clearly taught that any person may come to a sufficient understanding of them. (b) (c)

(a) As he does in all his letters when he speaks in them of these matters. There are some things in them that are hard to understand, which the ignorant and unstable twist to their own destruction, as they do the other Scriptures (2 Pet 3:16).

(b) The law of the LORD is perfect, reviving the soul; the testimony of the LORD is sure, making wise the simple; (Ps 19:7).

(c) The unfolding of your words gives light; it imparts understanding to the simple (Ps 119:130).

REMARKS: From the opening sentence of the Bible, "In the beginning God," we find the simplicity of Holy Scripture revealing the origins of the universe. God's Word gives light to those who earnestly seek the truth, enough so that even the simplest mind can know what God requires of him to gain entrance into heaven.

QUESTION 1–8: WHAT IS THE INFALLIBLE RULE OF INTERPRETING SCRIPTURE?

ANSWER: The single infallible rule to understand the Bible properly is to interpret Scripture with clearer passages. *(a)*

(a) Knowing this first of all, that no prophecy of Scripture comes from someone's own interpretation. For no prophecy was ever produced by the will of man, but men spoke from God as they were carried along by the Holy Spirit (2 Pet 1:20–21).

REMARKS: Some have argued that the Protestant Reformation was a war waged against corruption of biblical exegesis and interpretation. The Reformers exegeted Scripture by putting Christ at the center when reading each passage. This interpretive principle ultimately sprouted the movement to recover doctrinal purity within the church. The Reformers were constantly contending for the faith by bringing every doctrine under the scrutiny of other passages that spoke more clearly to the issue in question. In this manner, they were able to stand confidently in knowing their doctrines were truly Christ-centric and were compatible with the true teaching of Scripture.

QUESTION 1–9: WHAT IS THE FINAL AUTHORITY IN ALL MATTERS OF RELIGIOUS CONTROVERSIES?

ANSWER: The supreme judge that supersedes all decrees, opinions of writers and doctrines of men is the Holy Bible. *(a) (b) (c)*

(a) But Jesus answered them, "You are wrong, because you know neither the Scriptures nor the power of God" (Matt 22:29).

(b) And as for the resurrection of the dead, have you not read what was said to you by God (Matt 22:31).

(c) When they had appointed a day for him, they came to him at his lodging in greater numbers. From morning till evening he expounded to them, testifying to the kingdom of God and trying to convince them about Jesus both from the Law of Moses and from the Prophets (Acts 28:23).

REMARKS: Jesus Christ held his hearers accountable for what was revealed in Scripture. The God-breathed revelation was the standard upon which Jesus told individuals they were to be judged and not on the traditions of the forefathers. Although traditions, councils, and creeds are helpful to gain insight, only the Word of God holds the believer's conscience captive. God's Word is the standard and should not be subordinated to traditions of men (Matt 15:9).

2

God and the Trinity

QUESTION 2–1: WHO IS GOD?

ANSWER: The Lord our God is the one and only living and true God. *(a) (b) (c)*

   (a) Hear, O Israel: The LORD our God, the LORD is one (Deut 6:4).

   (b) Therefore, as to the eating of food offered to idols, we know that "an idol has no real existence," and that "there is no God but one" (1 Cor 8:4).

   (c) Yet for us there is one God, the Father, from whom are all things and for whom we exist, and one Lord, Jesus Christ, through whom are all things and through whom we exist (1 Cor 8:6).

REMARKS: It sounds simplistic to say that God is great, but the reality is that words fail to grasp the truth of who he is. God cannot be contained or fully understood in our finite minds. This, however, is not to imply that we do not have the capacity to know the truth of who he is. God condescended to our level through his Word and his Son so that we may understand him and give him the praise and glory he deserves.

QUESTION 2–2: WHAT HAS GOD REVEALED ABOUT HIMSELF TO US?

ANSWER: God is infinite in his being and perfection, whose essence cannot be comprehended by any but himself; *(a)* a pure spirit, *(b)* invisible, without body, parts, or passions, immortal, dwelling in the light which no one can approach unto. *(c)* He is without change, *(d)* immense, *(e)* eternal, *(f)* almighty, *(g)* most holy, *(h)* absolute and working all things according to the counsel of his own righteous will for his glory. *(i) (j)*

(a) God said to Moses, "I AM WHO I AM." And he said, "Say this to the people of Israel, 'I AM has sent me to you'" (Ex 3:14).

(b) "God is spirit, and those who worship him must worship in spirit and truth" (John 4:24).

(c) To the King of ages, immortal, invisible, the only God, be honor and glory forever and ever. Amen (1 Tim 1:17).

(d) "For I the LORD do not change; therefore you, O children of Jacob, are not consumed" (Mal 3:6).

(e) But will God indeed dwell on the earth? Behold, heaven and the highest heaven cannot contain you; how much less this house that I have built (1 Kings 8:27)!

(f) Before the mountains were brought forth, or ever you had formed the earth and the world, from everlasting to everlasting you are God (Ps 90:2).

(g) When Abram was ninety-nine years old the LORD appeared to Abram and said to him, "I am God Almighty; walk before me, and be blameless" (Gen 17:1).

(h) And one called to another and said: "Holy, holy, holy is the LORD of hosts; the whole earth is full of his glory" (Isaiah 6:3)!

(i) Our God is in the heavens; he does all that he pleases (Ps 115:3).

(j) Declaring the end from the beginning and from ancient times things not yet done, saying, "My counsel shall stand, and I will accomplish all my purpose" (Isa 46:10).

REMARKS: The Bible uses anthropomorphic language to describe God—which is ascribing human characteristics to God—so we can better understand him. Scripture paints a picture of God as having a face (Ex 33:11), ears (Neh 1:6), eyes (Job 28:10), and feet (Nah 1:3). This is not an actual portrayal of what God is, but rather, how he relates to us, his creation. God communicates indescribable truths about who he is in language we can understand.

Question 2–3: Upon whom does God depend?

Answer: God is unto himself all sufficient, not standing in need of any person which he created, nor deriving any glory from them. *(a)*

(a) Can a man be profitable to God? Surely he who is wise is profitable to himself. Is it any pleasure to the Almighty if you are in the right, or is it gain to him if you make your ways blameless (Job 22:2-3)?

Remarks: It is hard to imagine something without a beginning, yet this is exactly how the Bible describes God's eternal presence. He had no beginning, because he has always been in existence. This is important because his eternal being demonstrates he needs nothing outside of himself. The doctrine of self–existence is the foundation of how we think about him and how we understand his absolute being.

Question 2–4: How many persons are in the Godhead?

Answer: In the divine and infinite Being there are three persons, the Father, the Son (or Word), and the Holy Spirit. *(a) (b) (c)*

(a) Go therefore and make disciples of all nations, baptizing them in the name of the Father and of the Son and of the Holy Spirit (Matt 28:19).

(b) The grace of the Lord Jesus Christ and the love of God and the fellowship of the Holy Spirit be with you all (2 Cor 13:14).

(c) For there are three that testify (1 John 5:7).

Remarks: One of the most difficult doctrines to understand is the Trinity. Christians have been often accused of worshipping more than one God. This is partly because the human mind is unable to comprehend the greatness of God. The best we can do is come up with analogies to explain the Trinity but even this cannot begin to grasp the profound truths. The illustration many have used to explain one substance in three forms—water, steam, and ice—can not compare with God and the Trinity. We use language and our limited understanding to say that the Scriptures reveal to us a God who is one Being in three persons—Father, Son, and Holy Spirit.

QUESTION 2–5: WHAT IS THE RELATIONSHIP OF EACH PERSON IN THE GODHEAD?

ANSWER: The divine Being is of one substance, power, and eternity, each person having the whole divine essence, yet the essence undivided. *(a) (b) (c)*

(a) God said to Moses, "I AM WHO I AM." And he said, "Say this to the people of Israel, 'I AM has sent me to you'" (Ex 3:14).

(b) Believe me that I am in the Father and the Father is in me, or else believe on account of the works themselves (John 14:11).

(c) Yet for us there is one God, the Father, from whom are all things and for whom we exist, and one Lord, Jesus Christ, through whom are all things and through whom we exist (1 Cor 8:6).

REMARKS: One of the Trinitarian heresies the early church faced was modalism. This idea accepted the truth of the one true God but denied separate persons of the Godhead. Modalism taught the Father is the Son, the Son is the Spirit, and the Spirit is the Father. It is as if God assumes different roles. The illustration is sometimes used of a man being a father to his son, a son to his own father, and a husband to his wife. In this manner, he is able to fulfill three separate roles while still remaining one person. The problem modalism presents is that the Bible teaches three separate and distinct persons, each being coequal and co-eternal with the others, yet sharing one Being.

3

God's Decrees

QUESTION 3–1: WHAT HAS GOD DECREED?

ANSWER: God has decreed in himself, from all eternity, freely and unchangeably, all things which come to pass. *(a) (b) (c)*

(a) Declaring the end from the beginning and from ancient times things not yet done, saying, "My counsel shall stand, and I will accomplish all my purpose" (Isa 46:10).

(b) In him we have obtained an inheritance, having been predestined according to the purpose of him who works all things according to the counsel of his will (Eph 1:11).

(c) So when God desired to show more convincingly to the heirs of the promise the unchangeable character of his purpose, he guaranteed it with an oath (Heb 6:17).

REMARKS: Predestination is the biblical term used to signify God's predetermining or foreordaining the ultimate destiny of every individual. God's decision was made in eternity past and includes his decision to save some from eternal damnation (election) and to leave others in their sin (reprobation). Scripture does not reveal why God chose some to salvation, but the Bible is clear in that he predestined so that his purpose in election would stand (Rom 9:11) and to show the immeasurable riches of his grace in kindness towards us (Eph 2:7).

QUESTION 3–2: DOES PREDESTINATION MAKE GOD THE AUTHOR OF SIN?

ANSWER: God is neither the author of sin nor does he have fellowship with evil. *(a) (b) (a)* Let no one say when he is tempted, I am being tempted by God; for God cannot be tempted by evil, and he himself tempts no one (Jas 1:13).

(b) This is the message we have heard from him and proclaim to you, that God is light, and in him is no darkness at all (1 John 1:5).

REMARKS: The historic Reformed position has always been that God is not the author of evil but that he uses secondary causes to achieve his ends. However, it is not as if God did not want sin to come into existence. God's will was that sin should enter the world for his ultimate glory, otherwise it would have never happened. And it was more than bare permission—it was by God's eternal decree in order to fulfill his purpose. If God was not in absolute control over evil then we would have no assurance that he could prevent sinful actions from happening. If God did not ordain every evil act—past, present, and future—then there is no redemptive purpose why evil occurs. But, we know that God uses all sinful actions for his ultimate glory, just as Joseph told his brothers: "As for you, you meant evil against me, but God meant it for good, to bring it about that many people should be kept alive, as they are today" (Gen 50:20).

QUESTION 3-3: ARE GOD'S DECREES BASED ON FORESEEN EVENTS?

ANSWER: Although God knows everything that shall come to pass, *(a)* he has not decreed anything because he foresaw it as future, or as that which would come to pass upon given conditions. *(b) (c) (d)*

(a) Known unto God are all his works from the beginning of the world (Acts 15:18 KJV).

(b) Though they were not yet born and had done nothing either good or bad—in order that God's purpose of election might continue, not because of works but because of him who calls (Rom 9:11).

(c) So then it depends not on human will or exertion, but on God, who has mercy (Rom 9:16).

(d) So then he has mercy on whomever he wills, and he hardens whomever he wills (Rom 9:18).

REMARKS: Some have suggested that God's election is based on his foreknowledge of those who would accept him as Savior when given the chance. There are two main problems with this belief: it cannot be supported in Scripture, and it ignores the biblical view of man since the fall. Paul writes, "None is righteous, no, not one; no one understands; no one seeks for God" (Rom 3:10). Foreknowledge in the Bible refers to God's special love he had for his people before the foundation of the world.

QUESTION 3–4: DOES GOD ORDAIN SALVATION?

ANSWER: Some men and angels are predestined to eternal life through Jesus Christ *(a) (b)* to the praise of his glorious grace, *(c)* while others are left to revel in their own sin to their just condemnation. *(d) (e)*

(a) In the presence of God and of Christ Jesus and of the elect angels I charge you to keep these rules without prejudging, doing nothing from partiality (1 Tim 5:21).

(b) Then the King will say to those on his right, "Come, you who are blessed by my Father, inherit the kingdom prepared for you from the foundation of the world" (Matt 25:34).

(c) He predestined us for adoption as sons through Jesus Christ, according to the purpose of his will, to the praise of his glorious grace, with which he has blessed us in the Beloved (Eph 1:5–6).

(d) What if God, desiring to show his wrath and to make known his power, has endured with much patience vessels of wrath prepared for destruction (Rom 9:22).

(e) For certain people have crept in unnoticed who long ago were designated for this condemnation, ungodly people, who pervert the grace of our God into sensuality and deny our only Master and Lord, Jesus Christ (Jude 1:4).

REMARKS: God deals with people in two ways. He grants mercy to some and rewards justice to others. The Bible reminds us that we are all born into sin (Rom 5:12) and therefore all deserve death (Rom 6:23). God is under no obligation to save anyone, yet because of his mercy he has chosen to express free and sovereign grace to redeem a people for himself. Paul seems to address this very issue to the imaginary objector when he asked if election made God unjust, to which he responded "by no means" (Rom 9:14)! Paul continued, "I will have mercy on whom I will have mercy, and I will have compassion on whom I have compassion" (Rom 9:15).

QUESTION 3–5: WHEN DID GOD ORDAIN THE SALVATION OF THE ELECT?

ANSWER: God predestined mankind to salvation before the foundation of the world, according to his eternal and immutable purpose for the pleasure of his will. *(a) (b)*

(a) Even as he chose us in him before the foundation of the world, that we should be holy and blameless before him. In love he predestined us for adoption as sons through Jesus Christ, according to the purpose of his will (Eph 1:4–5).

(b) Making known to us the mystery of his will, according to his purpose, which he set forth in Christ (Eph 1:9).

REMARKS: The book of Revelation describes Jesus as being slain from the foundation of the world (Rev 13:8). This passage speaks to God's grace in his eternal election of sinners and provides a guarantee of heavenly citizenship. Since this sacrifice was made from the foundation of the world, it points out that the Old Testament saints are washed in the same blood as are New Testament believers. The desired effect of Christ's sacrifice is not limited by time but applies to every believer who has ever lived.

QUESTION 3–6: WHAT CAUSED GOD TO ORDAIN MANKIND UNTO SALVATION?

ANSWER: God elected some sinners unto salvation out of his free grace and love, *(a)* without any other thing in the creature as a condition or cause moving him to chose the way he did. *(b) (c)*

(a) Who saved us and called us to a holy calling, not because of our works but because of his own purpose and grace, which he gave us in Christ Jesus before the ages began (1 Tim 1:9).

(b) So then it depends not on human will or exertion, but on God, who has mercy (Rom 9:16).

(c) Even when we were dead in our trespasses, made us alive to-gether with Christ—by grace you have been saved (Eph 2:5).

REMARKS: Predestination and election do not absolve believers from their responsibility to make their calling and election sure (2 Pet 1:10), nor does it negate the biblical mandate to work out salvation with fear and trembling (Phil 2:12). Scripture tells us this can be accomplished by being thankful for our salvation (1 Tim 2:12), learning the will of God (Eph 5:17), and presenting ourselves as a living sacrifice (Rom 12:1). If we do these things we can be confident in our security, be-cause salvation is known by its fruit.

QUESTION 3–7: DID GOD ORDAIN ANYTHING ELSE ABOUT THE SALVIFIC PROCESS?

ANSWER: Just as God appointed the elect unto glory, so too did he foreordain the means to achieve salvation. *(a)* The elect, who fell in Adam and have been redeemed by Christ, *(b)* are effectually called unto faith in Christ, by his Spirit working in due season are justified, adopted, sanctified, *(c)* and are preserved by his power through faith unto salvation. *(d)*

(a) But we ought always to give thanks to God for you, brothers beloved by the Lord, because God chose you as the firstfruits to be saved, through sanctification by the Spirit and belief in the truth (2 Thess 2:13).

(b) For God has not destined us for wrath, but to obtain salvation through our Lord Jesus Christ, who died for us so that whether we are awake or asleep we might live with him (1 Thess 5:9–10).

(c) And those whom he predestined he also called, and those whom he called he also justified, and those whom he justified he also glorified (Rom 8:30).

(d) Who by God's power are being guarded through faith for a sal-vation ready to be revealed in the last time (1 Pet 1:5).

REMARKS: Jonah declared that salvation is of the Lord (Jon 2:9). No part in the salvific process belongs to man. He does not cooperate with God's grace to accept or to reject Christ unto salvation. If he did, then his salvation would be attributed in part to the fact that he was more spiritual, more intelligent, or wiser in choosing Christ than his neighbor who rejected the gospel. If salvation requires any cooperation on man's part—no matter how minute—salvation is no longer of grace.

QUESTION 3-8: WHAT IS THE VALUE OF STUDYING THIS DOCTRINE?

ANSWER: This doctrine provides a matter of praise, *(a) (b)* reverence, and admiration of God, and of humility, *(c) (d)* diligence, and abundant consolation to all that sincerely obey the gospel. *(e)*

(a) To the praise of his glorious grace, with which he has blessed us in the Beloved (Eph 1:6).

(b) Oh, the depth of the riches and wisdom and knowledge of God! How unsearchable are his judgments and how inscrutable his ways (Rom 11:33)!

(c) So too at the present time there is a remnant, chosen by grace. But if it is by grace, it is no longer on the basis of works; otherwise grace would no longer be grace (Rom 11:5-6).

(d) That is true. They were broken off because of their unbelief, but you stand fast through faith. So do not become proud, but fear (Rom 11:20).

(e) "Nevertheless, do not rejoice in this, that the spirits are subject to you, but rejoice that your names are written in heaven" (Luke 10:20).

REMARKS: Many have charged that teaching predestination and election causes needless division, but this should not deter Christians from contending for the faith (Jude 1:3). We are commanded to have a mature understanding of biblical doctrine. When understood properly, these truths deepen our respect of God's sovereignty. Predestination and election display his wisdom involving sin and help us understand that God alone truly saves. Furthermore, they reveal our fallen position while providing consolation that God's sure triumph over evil will be absolute.

4

Creation

Question 4-1: Who created all things?

ANSWER: In the beginning it pleased God the Father, Son, and Holy Spirit *(a) (b) (c)* to create the world and all things therein and all was very good. *(d)* God created for the displaying of the glory of his eternal power. *(e)*

> *(a)* He was in the beginning with God. All things were made through him, and without him was not any thing made that was made (John 1:2–3).

> *(b)* But in these last days he has spoken to us by his Son, whom he appointed the heir of all things, through whom also he created the world (Heb 1:2).

> *(c)* By his wind the heavens were made fair; his hand pierced the fleeing serpent (Job 26:13).

> *(d)* And God saw everything that he had made, and behold, it was very good. And there was evening and there was morning, the sixth day (Gen 1:31).

> *(e)* For his invisible attributes, namely, his eternal power and divine nature, have been clearly perceived, ever since the creation of the world, in the things that have been made. So they are without excuse (Rom 1:20).

REMARKS: Many Christians have tried to break the tension between a literal interpretation of Genesis and modern science with respect to the origins of the universe. They do so by claiming Genesis is concerned about who created and why, not about how and when. The reality is that such thinking is a tacit assault on the concept of being made in the image of God and of federal headship as it relates to original sin. Paul affirmed his belief in the literal interpretation of Genesis when he wrote that evil entered the world through the historical figure Adam (Rom 5:12).

QUESTION 4–2: HOW WAS MAN CREATED IN HIS ORIGINAL STATE?

ANSWER: God created male and female *(a)* with reasonable and immortal souls, *(b)* being made in the image of God, in knowledge, righteousness, and holiness, *(c) (d)* with the law of God written in their hearts, *(e)* and power to fulfill it, and yet under a possibility of sinning, being left to the liberty of their own will, which was subject to change. *(f)*

(a) So God created man in his own image, in the image of God he created him; male and female he created them (Gen 1:27).

(b) Then the LORD God formed the man of dust from the ground and breathed into his nostrils the breath of life, and the man became a living creature (Gen 2:7).

(c) Then God said, "Let us make man in our image, after our likeness. And let them have dominion over the fish of the sea and over the birds of the heavens and over the livestock and over all the earth and over every creeping thing that creeps on the earth" (Gen 1:26).

(d) See, this alone I found, that God made man upright, but they have sought out many schemes (Eccl 7:29).

(e) For when Gentiles, who do not have the law, by nature do what the law requires, they are a law to themselves, even though they do not have the law. They show that the work of the law is written on their hearts, while their conscience also bears witness, and their conflicting thoughts accuse or even excuse them (Rom 2:14–15).

(f) So when the woman saw that the tree was good for food, and that it was a delight to the eyes, and that the tree was to be desired to make one wise, she took of its fruit and ate, and she also gave some to her husband who was with her, and he ate (Gen 3:6).

REMARKS: The question of what it means to be made in the image of God has caused much debate and disagreement throughout Christendom. While the Scriptures may not be altogether clear on this issue, the text helps us define it. Man was endowed with an intellectual capacity to reason, moral uprightness, a human body, and dominion over the creation.

QUESTION 4–3: WHAT PROHIBITION WAS PLACED ON MAN?

ANSWER: Man received a command not to eat of the tree of knowledge of good and evil, *(a)* which so long as he obeyed, he was happy in his communion with God, and had dominion over the creatures. *(b) (c)*

> *(a)* "But of the tree of the knowledge of good and evil you shall not eat, for in the day that you eat of it you shall surely die" (Gen 2:17).

> *(b)* Then God said, "Let us make man in our image, after our likeness. And let them have dominion over the fish of the sea and over the birds of the heavens and over the livestock and over all the earth and over every creeping thing that creeps on the earth" (Gen 1:26).

> *(c)* And God blessed them. And God said to them, "Be fruitful and multiply and fill the earth and subdue it and have dominion over the fish of the sea and over the birds of the heavens and over every living thing that moves on the earth" (Gen 1:28).

REMARKS: The first covenant God made with man was a covenant of works. Adam represented all of mankind as the federal head. The terms of the covenant promised eternal life for obedience and guaranteed death for disobeying. When Adam broke the covenant, he and all his posterity stood condemned. Mankind was in need of redemption, and it was ultimately through a covenant of grace that Jesus Christ fulfilled the exacting requirements of the covenant of works on our behalf.

5

Providence

QUESTION 5-1: TO WHAT EXTENT IS GOD INVOLVED IN THE
AFFAIRS OF THE WORLD?

ANSWER: God the good Creator of all things, in His infinite power
and wisdom, upholds, directs, disposes, and governs all creatures and
things, *(a) (b)* from the greatest to the least. *(c)*

   (a) He is the radiance of the glory of God and the exact imprint of
   his nature, and he upholds the universe by the word of his power.
   After making purification for sins, he sat down at the right hand
   of the Majesty on high (Heb 1:3).

   (b) Declaring the end from the beginning and from ancient times
   things not yet done, saying, "My counsel shall stand, and I will accomplish all my purpose" calling a bird of prey from the east, the
   man of my counsel from a far country. I have spoken, and I will
   bring it to pass; I have purposed, and I will do it (Isa 46:10–11).

   (c) Are not two sparrows sold for a penny? And not one of them will
   fall to the ground apart from your Father. But even the hairs of
   your head are all numbered. Fear not, therefore; you are of more
   value than many sparrows (Matt 10:29–31).

REMARKS: Sovereignty is a natural element of God. It would be a contradiction in terms to speak of a God who is not sovereign over every
aspect of life. Simple logic confirms this with the law of non–contradiction. This truism tells us that something cannot be nothing and
something at the same time. Just as two plus two cannot equal four
and not equal four, God cannot be both sovereign over everything
and not be sovereign over everything. If we believe that we serve a

sovereign God then it stands to reason that he is in direct control over every event in this world to the smallest detail.

QUESTION 5-2: IS THE SOVEREIGNTY OF GOD RESTRICTED AT ALL BY HIS CREATION?

ANSWER: God makes use of means, *(a) (b) (c)* yet he is free to work without, *(d)* above, *(e)* and against them *(f)* at his pleasure.

(a) Paul said to the centurion and the soldiers, "Unless these men stay in the ship, you cannot be saved" (Acts 27:31).

(b) And the rest on planks or on pieces of the ship. And so it was that all were brought safely to land (Acts 27:44).

(c) "For as the rain and the snow come down from heaven and do not return there but water the earth, making it bring forth and sprout, giving seed to the sower and bread to the eater,11so shall my word be that goes out from my mouth; it shall not return to me empty, but it shall accomplish that which I purpose, and shall succeed in the thing for which I sent it" (Isa 55:10–11).

(d) But I will have mercy on the house of Judah, and I will save them by the LORD their God. I will not save them by bow or by sword or by war or by horses or by horsemen (Hos 1:7).

(e) He did not weaken in faith when he considered his own body, which was as good as dead (since he was about a hundred years old), or when he considered the barrenness of Sarah's womb. No distrust made him waver concerning the promise of God, but he grew strong in his faith as he gave glory to God, fully convinced that God was able to do what he had promised (Rom 4:19–21).

(f) And the satraps, the prefects, the governors, and the king's counselors gathered together and saw that the fire had not had any power over the bodies of those men. The hair of their heads was not singed, their cloaks were not harmed, and no smell of fire had come upon them (Dan 3:27).

REMARKS: The classic example of God's predestinating power and man's free will working together to accomplish the Lord's will is the biblical account of Judas and his betrayal of Jesus Christ. Judas acted freely when he delivered his Master to the Roman authorities for 30 pieces of silver so "that the Scripture might be fulfilled" (John 17:12). Even though God predestined the life, betrayal, death, and resurrection of his son, Jesus Christ, it would not have happened without the free decisions of everyone involved from Judas who freely betrayed Jesus to the Roman authorities who crucified Jesus willingly.

QUESTION 5–3: IS GOD SOVEREIGN OVER SIN?

ANSWER: God's sovereignty extends to the first fall and to all other sinful actions both of men and angels. *(a) (b) (c)* Sin's entrance into the world was not by a bare permission but was ordered and is governed by God, *(d) (e)* yet so the sinful acts proceed from the creatures and not from God who is not the author of sin. *(f) (g)*

(a) For God has consigned all to disobedience, that he may have mercy on all (Rom 11:32).

(b) Again the anger of the LORD was kindled against Israel, and he incited David against them, saying, "Go, number Israel and Judah" (2 Sam 24:1).

(c) Then Satan stood against Israel and incited David to number Israel (1 Chr 21:1).

(d) Because you have raged against me and your complacency has come into my ears, I will put my hook in your nose and my bit in your mouth, and I will turn you back on the way by which you came (2 King 19:28).

(e) Surely the wrath of man shall praise you; the remnant of wrath you will put on like a belt (Ps 76:10).

(f) These things you have done, and I have been silent; you thought that I was one like yourself. But now I rebuke you and lay the charge before you (Ps 50:21).

(g) For all that is in the world—the desires of the flesh and the desires of the eyes and pride in possessions—is not from the Father but is from the world (1 John 2:16).

REMARKS: The Bible says that God ordains evil to bring punishment upon the wicked (Ps 81:11–12), to bring good from it (Gen 50:20), and to test and discipline those he loves (Heb 12:4–14). Every sin that is committed has a special purpose in God's design which he is working out for good for those who love him (Rom 8:28).

QUESTION 5-4: WHY DOES GOD ALLOW BELIEVERS TO BACKSLIDE?

ANSWER: God sometimes leaves his saints for a short time to various temptations and the corruption of their own heart to chastise them for former sins, to show the depravity of the heart, to induce humility, and to arouse a dependence upon God alone for support. The desired result is to make them more watchful against future occasions of sin. *(a) (b) (c)*

(a) But Hezekiah did not make return according to the benefit done to him, for his heart was proud. Therefore wrath came upon him and Judah and Jerusalem. But Hezekiah humbled himself for the pride of his heart, both he and the inhabitants of Jerusalem, so that the wrath of the LORD did not come upon them in the days of Hezekiah (2 Chr 32:25–26).

(b) And so in the matter of the envoys of the princes of Babylon, who had been sent to him to inquire about the sign that had been done in the land, God left him to himself, in order to test him and to know all that was in his heart (2 Chr 32:31).

(c) So to keep me from becoming conceited because of the surpassing greatness of the revelations, a thorn was given me in the flesh, a messenger of Satan to harass me, to keep me from becoming conceited. Three times I pleaded with the Lord about this, that it should leave me. But he said to me, "My grace is sufficient for you, for my power is made perfect in weakness." Therefore I will boast all the more gladly of my weaknesses, so that the power of Christ may rest upon me (2 Cor 12:7–9).

REMARKS: The Lord promised his people that he would circumcise their hearts (Deut 30:6). This was a covenant between God and man that was not conditional. God did not make his vow dependant upon human effort, but instead made the positive statement that he would give his elect a new heart and he would be there God (Jer 32:38–39). This demonstrates the depth of God's mercy to his people in that he is constantly abiding even though the natural tendency is to constantly wander away from him.

QUESTION 5-5: HOW DOES GOD HARDEN THE HEARTS OF INDIVIDUALS?

ANSWER: God is free to withhold his grace from men whereby they have not been enlightened in their understanding, *(a)* and exposes them to such circumstances that their own corruption produces them to sin. *(b) (c)*

- *(a)* But to this day the LORD has not given you a heart to understand or eyes to see or ears to hear (Deut 29:4).

- *(b)* But Sihon the king of Heshbon would not let us pass by him, for the LORD your God hardened his spirit and made his heart obstinate, that he might give him into your hand, as he is this day (Deut 2:30).

- *(c)* And Hazael said, "Why does my lord weep?" He answered, "Because I know the evil that you will do to the people of Israel. You will set on fire their fortresses, and you will kill their young men with the sword and dash in pieces their little ones and rip open their pregnant women." And Hazael said, 'What is your servant, who is but a dog, that he should do this great thing?' Elisha answered, "The LORD has shown me that you are to be king over Syria" (2 Kings 8:12–13).

REMARKS: God does not force any person to sin against his own will, but he does allow the true nature of the heart to be revealed. God hardens the heart by withdrawing his grace, and when he does, this leaves the unbeliever in an inevitable situation whereby he will naturally and willingly follow the evil inclinations of his heart. It is in this manner that God hardens hearts.

QUESTION 5-6: WHAT COMFORT DOES THE DOCTRINE OF GOD'S PROVIDENCE BRING?

ANSWER: God's providence reaches to all his creation, including taking care of his church and granting all things good to it for his glory. *(a) (b) (c)*

(a) For to this end we toil and strive, because we have our hope set on the living God, who is the Savior of all people, especially of those who believe (1 Tim 4:10).

(b) "Behold, the eyes of the Lord GOD are upon the sinful kingdom, and I will destroy it from the surface of the ground, except that I will not utterly destroy the house of Jacob," declares the LORD. "For behold, I will command, and shake the house of Israel among all the nations as one shakes with a sieve, but no pebble shall fall to the earth" (Amos 9:8–9).

(c) For I am the LORD your God, the Holy One of Israel, your Savior. I give Egypt as your ransom, Cush and Seba in exchange for you. Because you are precious in my eyes, and honored, and I love you, I give men in return for you, peoples in exchange for your life. Fear not, for I am with you; I will bring your offspring from the east, and from the west I will gather you (Isa 43:3–5).

REMARKS: Believers can take comfort in knowing that they do not have to rely on blind fortune or good luck. God has ordained every event in this world to the smallest detail—even the most horrific sin against the Christian. It is hard for many to imagine that God ordains evil as well as good works, but it should provide Christians comfort to know that there are no purposeless acts. All evil will be redeemed for good. So, everything that happens to the believer is ultimately for his spiritual and eternal good (Rom 8:28).

6

Sin and Punishment

QUESTION 6-1: HOW DID MAN FALL FROM A STATE OF INNOCENCE?

ANSWER: Satan used the subtlety of the serpent to tempt Eve, who then seduced Adam into sinning. Adam willfully broke the law of their creation and the command given to them by eating the forbidden fruit. *(a) (b)*

> *(a)* The man said, "The woman whom you gave to be with me, she gave me fruit of the tree, and I ate." Then the LORD God said to the woman, "What is this that you have done?" The woman said, "The serpent deceived me, and I ate" (Gen 3:12–13).

> *(b)* But I am afraid that as the serpent deceived Eve by his cunning, your thoughts will be led astray from a sincere and pure devotion to Christ (2 Cor 11:3).

REMARKS: St. Augustine, bishop of Hippo, first gave Christendom the term original sin. It is not a phrase that can be found in Scripture, but it is an expression that adequately exposes the reality of sin in our spiritual system. Simply put, original sin means that sin taints everyone from birth, in that the heart, mind, and will have an inclination towards evil. We are not sinners because we sin, instead we sin because we are sinners. As the Psalmist wrote, "Behold, I was brought forth in iniquity, and in sin did my mother conceive me" (Ps 51:5).

QUESTION 6–2: WHAT HAPPENED AS A RESULT OF ADAM'S SIN?

ANSWER: Death came upon all mankind as a result of Adam's sin. *(a)* Everyone is now wholly defiled in all the faculties and parts of soul and body. *(b) (c) (d) (e) (f)*

(a) Therefore, just as sin came into the world through one man, and death through sin, and so death spread to all men because all sinned (Rom 5:12).

(b) For all have sinned and fall short of the glory of God (Rom 3:23).

(c) To the pure, all things are pure, but to the defiled and unbelieving, nothing is pure; but both their minds and their consciences are defiled (Tit 1:15).

(d) The LORD saw that the wickedness of man was great in the earth, and that every intention of the thoughts of his heart was only evil continually (Gen 6:5).

(e) The heart is deceitful above all things, and desperately sick; who can understand it (Jer 17:9)?

(f) As it is written: "None is righteous, no, not one; no one understands; no one seeks for God. All have turned aside; together they have become worthless; no one does good, not even one. Their throat is an open grave; they use their tongues to deceive. The venom of asps is under their lips. Their mouth is full of curses and bitterness. Their feet are swift to shed blood; in their paths are ruin and misery, and the way of peace they have not known. There is no fear of God before their eyes" (Rom 3:10–18).

REMARKS: Many critics of biblical infallibility have sought to reconcile Genesis with evolution, and by so doing, have cast doubt upon the literal interpretation of the creation narrative. The apostle Paul did not seem to question the historicity of Genesis when he taught sin entered the world through Adam (Rom 5:12). The Christian faith has always maintained that God made the first man the representative for all his posterity. God placed Adam in a position to choose between good and evil, and he chose the latter. Consequently, Adam's federal representation of the human race is the root cause of the transmission of sin to all mankind.

QUESTION 6-3: HOW DO PEOPLE ACT IN THEIR NATURAL STATE?

ANSWER: Man's nature from birth is utterly indisposed, disabled, and made opposite to all good, and wholly inclined to evil. *(a) (b)*

(a) For the mind that is set on the flesh is hostile to God, for it does not submit to God's law; indeed, it cannot (Rom 8:7).

(b) And you, who once were alienated and hostile in mind, doing evil deeds (Col 1:21).

REMARKS: The terms total depravity or radical depravity are commonly used to signify the extent of original sin. They express the complete inability of man to cooperate in any respect in his salvation because of the profound effect of sin. The fall from grace extended to all parts of man's being including the body, mind, and will—rendering him incapable of spiritual understanding and any love towards God. This doctrine is not meant to imply that individuals are as sinful as they could be. Radical depravity simply means that man does not have the ability to believe in God, because he is dead in his sin. God alone must first change the heart before one is able or desirous to believe.

QUESTION 6-4: DOES REGENERATION REMOVE THE INCLINATION TO SIN?

ANSWER: The corruption of the flesh remains in those who have been regenerated. *(a) (b) (c) (d)*

(a) For I know that nothing good dwells in me, that is, in my flesh. For I have the desire to do what is right, but not the ability to carry it out (Rom 7:18).

(b) But I see in my members another law waging war against the law of my mind and making me captive to the law of sin that dwells in my members (Rom 7:23).

(c) Surely there is not a righteous man on earth who does good and never sins (Eccl 7:20).

(d) If we say we have no sin, we deceive ourselves, and the truth is not in us (1 John 1:8).

REMARKS: Regeneration is the act of the Holy Spirit working within individuals to renew the heart, making it alive. This act is necessary, because Paul tells us by nature people are dead in their trespasses and sins. Jesus further taught that unless a sinner was regenerated or born again, he could not see the kingdom of heaven. Nevertheless, in spite of the fact that God renews the heart, the unfortunate reality is that we still retain our sinful nature. That is why we continue to sin despite having been regenerated. It will not be until that glorious day when the Lord gives us new bodies that we will be free from the effects of sin.

7

God's Covenant

QUESTION 7-1: CAN MAN DO ANYTHING TO EARN OR TO
MERIT SALVATION?

ANSWER: The distance between God and the creature is so great
that they never could have attained the reward of eternal life except
through the voluntary condescension by God, which he has been
pleased to express through a covenant. *(a) (b)*

(a) So you also, when you have done all that you were commanded,
say, "We are unworthy servants; we have only done what was our
duty" (Luke 17:10).

(b) If you are righteous, what do you give to him? Or what does he
receive from your hand? Your wickedness concerns a man like
yourself, and your righteousness a son of man (Job 35:7–8).

REMARKS: The covenant of redemption was the eternal agreement
between the Godhead in which the Father appointed his Son to redeem his chosen people. Some do not include the Holy Spirit in this
covenant because the condition of redemption was based upon the
Son's obligation to the Father. Nevertheless, the Holy Spirit's working
is essential in the salvific process, as he is the one who quickens the
dead and applies the work of Christ.

QUESTION 7-2: WHAT TYPE OF COVENANT DID GOD MAKE
WITH MAN?

ANSWER: The Lord made a covenant of grace with man after he
brought himself under the curse of the law by his fall. *(a) (b) (c)* In
this covenant the Lord freely offers to sinners life and salvation by

Jesus Christ, requiring from them faith in him that they may be saved. *(d) (e)*

> *(a)* "But of the tree of the knowledge of good and evil you shall not eat, for in the day that you eat of it you shall surely die" (Gen 2:17).

> *(b)* For all who rely on works of the law are under a curse; for it is written, "Cursed be everyone who does not abide by all things written in the Book of the Law, and do them" (Gal 3:10).

> *(c)* For by works of the law no human being will be justified in his sight, since through the law comes knowledge of sin. But now the righteousness of God has been manifested apart from the law, although the Law and the Prophets bear witness to it (Rom 3:20–21).

> *(d)* For God has done what the law, weakened by the flesh, could not do. By sending his own Son in the likeness of sinful flesh and for sin, he condemned sin in the flesh (Rom 8:3).

> *(e)* And he said to them, "Go into all the world and proclaim the gospel to the whole creation. Whoever believes and is baptized will be saved, but whoever does not believe will be condemned" (Mark 16:15–16).

REMARKS: Jesus promised his disciples before he died that he would send "another Helper" (John 14:16). What this meant was that the disciples would not be left alone in the world but would be provided with supernatural help for encouragement, edification, counsel and strength. Additionally, the Holy Spirit has a separate function with respect to salvation. The Spirit, who is coequal with the Father and the Son, works within unbelievers to reveal the truth to them and to give them a new heart and a new spirit (Ezek 36:26) so that they may believe and have faith unto eternal life.

QUESTION 7–3: HOW IS THE COVENANT OF GRACE
REVEALED?

ANSWER: The Lord's covenant with man is revealed through the
Gospel; first of all to Adam in the promise of salvation by the seed of
the woman, *(a)* and afterwards by further steps until the full revelation was completed in the New Testament. *(b)*

- *(a)* "I will put enmity between you and the woman, and between
  your offspring and her offspring; he shall bruise your head, and
  you shall bruise his heel" (Gen 3:15).

- *(b)* Long ago, at many times and in many ways, God spoke to our
  fathers by the prophets (Heb 1:1).

REMARKS: The Old Testament is replete with types and shadows, which
God used to prepare the nation of Israel for the coming Messiah.
When the time had come, Jesus Christ offered himself as the perfect
and final sacrifice for sin, serving as the Second Adam. This simply
means that Jesus acted as the representative to redeem mankind, just
as Adam served as the federal representative when he brought sin and
death to the entire human race. Christ's perfect fulfillment of the old
covenant opened the door to usher in the Gentiles by grace through
faith alone in Jesus Christ.

8

Christt the Mediator

QUESTION 8–1: WHAT FUNCTIONS DOES JESUS CHRIST FULFILL?

ANSWER: The Lord Jesus was chosen and ordained to be the mediator between God and man; *(a) (b)* the prophet, *(c)* priest, *(d)* and king; *(e) (f)* head and savior of his church, *(g)* the heir of all things, *(h)* and judge of the world. *(i)*

(a) Behold my servant, whom I uphold, my chosen, in whom my soul delights; I have put my Spirit upon him; he will bring forth justice to the nations (Isa 42:1).

(b) For there is one God, and there is one mediator between God and men, the man Christ Jesus (1 Tim 2:5).

(c) Moses said, "The Lord God will raise up for you a prophet like me from your brothers. You shall listen to him in whatever he tells you" (Acts 3:22).

(d) So also Christ did not exalt himself to be made a high priest, but was appointed by him who said to him, "You are my Son, today I have begotten you"; as he says also in another place, "You are a priest forever, after the order of Melchizedek" (Heb 5:5–6).

(e) "As for me, I have set my King on Zion, my holy hill" (Ps 2:6).

(f) "And he will reign over the house of Jacob forever, and of his kingdom there will be no end" (Luke 1:33).

(g) And he put all things under his feet and gave him as head over all things to the church, which is his body, the fullness of him who fills all in all (Eph 1:22–23).

(h) But in these last days he has spoken to us by his Son, whom he appointed the heir of all things, through whom also he created the world (Heb 1:2).

(i) "Because he has fixed a day on which he will judge the world in righteousness by a man whom he has appointed; and of this he has given assurance to all by raising him from the dead" (Acts 17:31).

REMARKS: John Calvin first brought the three–fold office of Jesus Christ into prominence in the development of his Christology. This view of Christ was representative of a prophet, priest, and king—who fulfilled all the anointed offices held in the Old Testament. What Calvin meant with the three–fold office is that Christ served as a representative of God to man (prophet), is currently interceding for us with God (priest), and has become the Lord over our lives (king).

QUESTION 8–2: IS JESUS GOD?

ANSWER: The Son of God, the second person in the Trinity, being true and eternal God, the brightness of the Father's glory, is of one substance and equal with him. *(a)* Yet, Jesus took upon him man's nature, with all the essential properties and weaknesses, *(b) (c)* yet without sin. *(d)*

(a) And we know that the Son of God has come and has given us understanding, so that we may know him who is true; and we are in him who is true, in his Son Jesus Christ. He is the true God and eternal life (1 John 5:20).

(b) And the Word became flesh and dwelt among us, and we have seen his glory, glory as of the only Son from the Father, full of grace and truth (John 1:14).

(c) But when the fullness of time had come, God sent forth his Son, born of woman, born under the law (Gal 4:4).

(d) For we do not have a high priest who is unable to sympathize with our weaknesses, but one who in every respect has been tempted as we are, yet without sin (Heb 4:15).

REMARKS: The Council of Nicaea (AD 325) defined the doctrine of the Trinity in response to the Arian controversy that taught there was a time when the Son was not in existence. The council affirmed that the Son was of the same substance or essence as God the Father. By declaring God and the Son to be "of one substance," and that the latter was "begotten, not made" the Nicene Creed unequivocally acknowledged both the humanity and deity of Jesus.

QUESTION 8–3: WHAT MAKES JESUS UNIQUE?

ANSWER: Jesus Christ has human and divine natures, making him both God and man yet being one person. *(a)*

(a) Thomas answered him, "My Lord and my God" (John 20:28)!

REMARKS: Many Christian heresies developed concerning the nature of Christ from sects that taught Jesus was purely human to others that believed Jesus was fully divine. Some of the more popular heresies included Sabellianism, which taught the Father, Son, and Holy Spirit were three modes or roles of the single person, God—implying Jesus Christ was purely divine. Docetism was a second heresy that denied the physical body of Christ. The name is derived from the Greek, which means "to seem." The Docetists believed the Jesus Christ did not have a real body, that he only seemed to be human. A third heresy from the early church was Apollinarianism. This heresy suggested that Jesus had a human body and soul but that his mind was taken over by the eternal Logos. Each of these heresies were condemned by the church who upheld the biblical view that Jesus is one person in two natures. That is to say, Jesus Christ is fully human and fully divine.

QUESTION 8–4: WHAT OFFICE DID JESUS WILLINGLY UNDERTAKE ON BEHALF OF THE ELECT?

ANSWER: Jesus perfectly fulfilled and underwent the punishment due to us, which we should have suffered, being made sin and a curse for us, *(a) (b) (c)* so that He might be raised from the dead to sit at the right hand of his Father and to make intercession for his people. *(d)*

(a) Christ redeemed us from the curse of the law by becoming a curse for us—for it is written, "Cursed is everyone who is hanged on a tree" (Gal 3:13).

(b) For Christ also suffered once for sins, the righteous for the un-righteous, that he might bring us to God, being put to death in the flesh but made alive in the spirit (1 Pet 3:18).

(c) For our sake he made him to be sin who knew no sin, so that in him we might become the righteousness of God (2 Cor 5:21).

(d) Who is to condemn? Christ Jesus is the one who died—more than that, who was raised—who is at the right hand of God, who indeed is interceding for us (Rom 8:34).

REMARKS: Definite redemption refers to the specific intent of the death of Jesus Christ on the cross. Simply put, this doctrine state that Christ accomplished what he came to earth to do: to save his people from their sins (Matt 1:21). This belief is in contrast to universalism, or the idea that Christ died for all of mankind without exception. The historic Reformed doctrine believes that Jesus' death was of infinite value, yet was only offered to save those whom the Father knew beforehand. In this manner, Jesus paid the penalty on behalf of the elect.

QUESTION 8–5: WHAT DID JESUS ACCOMPLISH THROUGH HIS SACRIFICE ON THE CROSS?

ANSWER: Jesus' sacrifice of himself on the cross fully satisfied the justice of God, (a) (b) procured reconciliation, and purchased an everlasting inheritance in the kingdom of heaven for all who have faith in Jesus Christ. (c) (d) (e)

(a) How much more will the blood of Christ, who through the eternal Spirit offered himself without blemish to God, purify our conscience from dead works to serve the living God (Heb 9:14).

(b) For by a single offering he has perfected for all time those who are being sanctified (Heb 10:14).

(c) Whom God put forward as a propitiation by his blood, to be received by faith. This was to show God's righteousness, because in his divine forbearance he had passed over former sins. It was to show his righteousness at the present time, so that he might be just and the justifier of the one who has faith in Jesus (Rom 3:25–26).

(d) Since you have given him authority over all flesh, to give eternal life to all whom you have given him (John 17:2).

(e) Therefore he is the mediator of a new covenant, so that those who are called may receive the promised eternal inheritance, since a death has occurred that redeems them from the transgressions committed under the first covenant (Heb 9:15).

REMARKS: Propitiation is one of those big theological words that many have heard but might not fully understand. The word is defined as the act of appeasing wrath and gaining the favor of an offended person. In theological terms, propitiation refers to the work of Jesus on the cross in that he bore our sin and guilt and paid the debt we owed God but were unable to pay. Jesus Christ faced the wrath of God in our place, and by acting as our substitute, he obtained the favor of God.

QUESTION 8–6: WERE OLD TESTAMENT BELIEVERS SAVED IN A DIFFERENT MANNER THAN NEW TESTAMENT BELIEVERS?

ANSWER: Every individual who enters the kingdom of heaven will be there because of faith in Christ Jesus. With that said, the price of redemption was not actually paid by Christ until after his incarnation. The desired result and benefit arising from his payment were communicated to the elect in all ages from the beginning of the world through those promises, types, and sacrifices in which he was revealed and signified as the seed which should bruise the serpent's head, (a) (b) and the Lamb slain from the foundation of the world. (c)

(a) For good news came to us just as to them, but the message they heard did not benefit them, because they were not united by faith with those who listened (Heb 4:2).

(b) Concerning this salvation, the prophets who prophesied about the grace that was to be yours searched and inquired carefully, inquiring what person or time the Spirit of Christ in them was indicating when he predicted the sufferings of Christ and the subsequent glories (1 Pet 1:10–11).

(c) And all who dwell on earth will worship it, everyone whose name has not been written before the foundation of the world in the book of life of the Lamb who was slain (Rev 13:8).

REMARKS: Some people falsely assume that the Old Testament believers were not saved by grace through faith alone. Instead, they presume that believers under the Old Covenant were saved by their obedience to the laws of Moses. The truth is that all believers in all generations are saved the same way: by grace, through faith alone, on the account of Christ alone. The Old Testament ceremonial, dietary, and sacrificial laws were temporary enactments for the purpose of instruction in pointing towards something greater to come. The Old Testament believers looked forward to the coming Messiah, the New Testament believers look back at the Messiah, but everyone looks towards the work of Christ on the cross for salvation.

QUESTION 8–7: WHAT WORK DOES JESUS DO ON BEHALF OF THE ELECT IN THE SALVIFIC PROCESS?

ANSWER: Jesus Christ makes intercession for his elect, *(a) (b) (c)* reveals unto them the mystery of salvation and persuades them to believe and obey. *(d) (e) (f)* Moreover, Christ overcomes all the enemies by his almighty power and wisdom. *(g) (h)*

(a) All that the Father gives me will come to me, and whoever comes to me I will never cast out (John 6:37).

(b) Just as the Father knows me and I know the Father; and I lay down my life for the sheep. And I have other sheep that are not of this fold. I must bring them also, and they will listen to my voice. So there will be one flock, one shepherd (John 10:15–16).

(c) I am praying for them. I am not praying for the world but for those whom you have given me, for they are yours (John 17:9).

(d) I have manifested your name to the people whom you gave me out of the world. Yours they were, and you gave them to me, and they have kept your word (John 17:6).

(e) Making known to us the mystery of his will, according to his purpose, which he set forth in Christ (Eph 1:9).

(f) And we know that the Son of God has come and has given us understanding, so that we may know him who is true; and we are in him who is true, in his Son Jesus Christ. He is the true God and eternal life (1 John 5:20).

(g) The LORD says to my Lord: "Sit at my right hand, until I make your enemies your footstool" (Ps 110:1).

(h) For he must reign until he has put all his enemies under his feet. The last enemy to be destroyed is death (1 Cor 15:25–26).

REMARKS: The word intercession means "to come between." In biblical usage, an intercessor is one who petitions God on behalf of someone else. The Old Testament high priest acted as an intercessor between the Israelites and God, but this only foreshadowed Jesus Christ who would be man's advocate with the Father in perpetuity (1 John 2:1).

QUESTION 8–8: CAN THERE BE MORE THAN ONE MEDIATOR?

ANSWER: The office of mediator between God and man belongs only to Christ, who is the prophet, priest, and king of the church of God. It may not be transferred in any part from him or shared by any other person. *(a)*

(a) For there is one God, and there is one mediator between God and men, the man Christ Jesus (1 Tim 2:5).

REMARKS: There is a movement afoot within Roman Catholicism that is ascribing to Mary the office of mediator—an office that the Bible attributes to Jesus Christ alone. It is believed that since Mary gave the source of all grace to men, it is only fitting that she would also be co–operator in the distribution of grace. Additionally, she is believed to be the spiritual mother of all the redeemed so her motherly intercession is not only logical, it is necessary. The problem, however, is that the Bible is clear with respect to this issue. Jesus Christ is the mediator of the new covenant (Heb 12:24), and it is only through him that we have salvation (Eph 2:7).

9

Free Will

QUESTION 9–1: HOW WAS THE WILL OF MAN CREATED?

ANSWER: God provided the will of man with the natural liberty and power of acting upon choice, that it is neither forced, nor by any necessity of nature determined to do good or evil. *(a) (b) (c)*

(a) "But I tell you that Elijah has already come, and they did not recognize him, but did to him whatever they pleased. So also the Son of Man will certainly suffer at their hands" (Matt 17:12).

(b) But each person is tempted when he is lured and enticed by his own desire (Jas 1:14).

(c) I call heaven and earth to witness against you today, that I have set before you life and death, blessing and curse. Therefore choose life, that you and your offspring may live (Deut 30:19).

REMARKS: Free will is defined in theological terms as the ability to choose any of the moral options in a given situation. Augustine taught extensively that this freedom of choice was lost through the fall since sin has corrupted the body, mind, and will. Natural man no longer has the freedom to choose between good and evil, nor does he have the inclination to do so because he is hostile towards God (Rom 8:7). This does not mean that man is unable to choose at all, it just means that when given the opportunity to choose between doing good or committing evil mankind will always choose the latter (Rom 3:10–18).

QUESTION 9–2: DID ADAM HAVE THE FREEDOM TO CHOOSE TO DO WHAT WAS PLEASING TO GOD?

ANSWER: Adam had freedom and power to will and to do that which was pleasing to God before the fall, *(a)* but he was also able to change by choice and fall from grace. *(b)*

> *(a)* See, this alone I found, that God made man upright, but they have sought out many schemes (Eccl 7:29).

> *(b)* So when the woman saw that the tree was good for food, and that it was a delight to the eyes, and that the tree was to be desired to make one wise, she took of its fruit and ate, and she also gave some to her husband who was with her, and he ate (Gen 3:6).

REMARKS: The mystery of how the first evil choice could voluntarily arise from a creature made perfect and holy will probably never be solved in this life. It is hard to imagine what would cause a creature to choose evil if he was not already inclined to do so. Theologians have debated this issue for centuries and have offered reasonable explanations. Finite creatures can only remain without blemish through the indwelling of a perpetually holy God guarding against sin. But, if God chose to remove his preserving power from his creatures they would inevitably fall. This is what happened with Satan and Adam causing each to rebel. By way of illustration, to make a candle burn—it must be lighted, and to make the flame go out—it only need to be left alone.

QUESTION 9–3: DID ADAM'S WILL CHANGE AFTER HE SINNED AGAINST GOD?

ANSWER: Because Adam fell into a state of sin, he wholly lost his ability to will to any spiritual good, which accompanies salvation. *(a) (b)*

> *(a)* For while we were still weak, at the right time Christ died for the ungodly (Rom 5:6).

> *(b)* For the mind that is set on the flesh is hostile to God, for it does not submit to God's law; indeed, it cannot (Rom 8:7).

REMARKS: The phrase total depravity is often used to describe man's condition after the fall. Some quickly object to this term and point out that many unbelievers do good works. That unsaved individuals perform good works is not in view when this theological phrase is used. What total depravity refers to is the extent to which the fall has left all men. Total depravity speaks to the total inability of man to believe in God or his Word apart from divine illumination.

QUESTION 9–4: WHAT IS THE PRESENT CONDITION OF MAN'S WILL?

ANSWER: Natural man is altogether opposed from good and is dead in sin. *(a) (b)*

(a) And you were dead in the trespasses and sins (Eph 2:1).

(b) Even when we were dead in our trespasses, made us alive together with Christ—by grace you have been saved (Eph 2:5).

REMARKS: Biblical anthropology is the study of man as described in Scripture. The Old Testament represents mankind as spiritually dead and in active rebellion towards God. The Psalmist describes the utter corruption of humanity as a world that refuses to seek after God because of selfishness (Ps 14). The New Testament is just as sobering when it describes man as "worthless" and "unrighteous" (Rom 3:10–18; Eph 2:1–3).

QUESTION 9–5: IF WE ARE DEAD TO SIN HOW IS ANYONE EVER SAVED?

ANSWER: When God converts a sinner, he translates him into a state of grace and frees him from his natural bondage under sin. *(a) (b)* God enables the sinner to will and to do that which is pleasing unto God. *(c) (d)*

(a) He has delivered us from the domain of darkness and transferred us to the kingdom of his beloved Son (Col 1:13).

(b) So if the Son sets you free, you will be free indeed (John 8:36).

(c) For it is God who works in you, both to will and to work for his good pleasure (Phil 2:13).

(d) And I will give you a new heart, and a new spirit I will put within you. And I will remove the heart of stone from your flesh and give you a heart of flesh. And I will put my Spirit within you, and cause you to walk in my statutes and be careful to obey my rules (Ezek 36:26–27).

REMARKS: The Gospel of Matthew assures us God will save his people from their sins (Matt 1:21). This is more than the mere promise of God saving us from the penalty of death. It is also assurance that he will deliver us from the power of sin and will eventually release us from the presence of sin by taking us from this world. The Lord accomplishes his will through the working of the Holy Spirit. The Bible teaches us the Spirit supernaturally works within us to make us alive in Christ by taking away our hearts of stone and giving us hearts of flesh (Ezek 36:26).

QUESTION 9–6: WHEN IS THE WILL TO BE MADE PERFECT?

ANSWER: The will of man will only be made perfect and immutably free to good alone in the state of glory. *(a)*

> *(a)* Until we all attain to the unity of the faith and of the knowledge of the Son of God, to mature manhood, to the measure of the stature of the fullness of Christ (Eph 4:13).

REMARKS: Many Christians have often wondered if it is possible for saints in heaven to loose their salvation. The simple answer is, "no" —no Christian who is in the presence of the Lord will ever fall from a state of grace. God's plan of salvation involves three steps: redemption, sanctification, and glorification. The latter is the transforming work that removes all sin from us and makes us fit to be in perfect communion with God. Furthermore, Christians have Jesus Christ as their intermediary who serves as a perpetual intercessor both in this world and the next. The Mediator Jesus Christ will loose no one (John 17).

10

Effectual Calling

QUESTION 10–1: WHAT IS EFFECTUAL CALLING?

ANSWER: It is the call by God's Word and Spirit out of a state of sin and death to grace and salvation by Jesus Christ. *(a) (b)*

 (a) "To open their eyes, so that they may turn from darkness to light and from the power of Satan to God, that they may receive forgiveness of sins and a place among those who are sanctified by faith in me" (Acts 26:18).

 (b) That the God of our Lord Jesus Christ, the Father of glory, may give you a spirit of wisdom and of revelation in the knowledge of him, having the eyes of your hearts enlightened, that you may know what is the hope to which he has called you, what are the riches of his glorious inheritance in the saints (Eph 1:17–18).

REMARKS: Effectual calling must be distinguished from the general calling. The latter goes out to everyone (Matt 22:14) but can be refused because of man's unresponsiveness and hardness of heart. Effectual calling will be effective because of the work of the Holy Spirit. He works inwardly to enlighten the mind and to renew the heart in those for whom God has a special love. This act performed by the Holy Spirit cannot fail to bring regeneration to God's people (John 10:3–4).

QUESTION 10–2: IS GOD'S EFFECTUAL CALLING INCUMBENT UPON FORESEEN FAITH?

ANSWER: God's effectual call is of grace alone and therefore not incumbent upon anything at all foreseen in man, nor from any power in the creature co–working with his special grace. *(a) (b)*

(a) Who saved us and called us to a holy calling, not because of our works but because of his own purpose and grace, which he gave us in Christ Jesus before the ages began (1 Tim 1:9).

(b) For by grace you have been saved through faith. And this is not your own doing; it is the gift of God (Eph 2:8).

REMARKS: Many have asserted that God's foreknowledge in election is based upon those who would choose Christ as their Savior. But this interpretation misses the understanding of the term translated as foreknow. This word goes beyond mere recognition. It expresses the idea of God's love for us and implies a special relationship. Opponents of the foreknowledge view also point out that sinners are naturally dead in sin, and are unable to repent apart from the Holy Spirit first making them alive. So, even if granted the opportunity to choose Christ, they would be unable and unwilling to do so because of their bondage to sin.

QUESTION 10–3: DO BABIES WHO DIE IN INFANCY ENTER HEAVEN?

ANSWER: Elect babies who die in infancy are regenerated and saved by Christ through the Holy Spirit, (a) even though they are incapable of being outwardly called by the ministry of the Word.

(a) But when Jesus saw it, he was indignant and said to them, "Let the children come to me; do not hinder them, for to such belongs the kingdom of God" (Mark 10:14).

REMARKS: There are two main passages that provide examples concerning infants and the possibility of a favorable standing before God. The first is that of John the Baptist being filled with the Holy Spirit while in his mother's womb (Luke 1:15). The second, and perhaps strongest argument for infant salvation, is David's statement after the death of his son: "I shall go to him, but he will not return to me" (2 Sam 12:23). David's agony was great, but he consoled himself in knowing that one day he would be reunited in heaven with his son.

QUESTION 10-4: WILL THOSE WHO HAVE NEVER HEARD THE GOSPEL MESSAGE GO TO HEAVEN?

ANSWER: Unless the Father effectually draws a person, he cannot come to Christ and therefore will not be saved. *(a) (b)*

(a) No one can come to me unless the Father who sent me draws him. And I will raise him up on the last day. It is written in the Prophets, "And they will all be taught by God." Everyone who has heard and learned from the Father comes to me (John 6:44–45).

(b) And he said, "This is why I told you that no one can come to me unless it is granted him by the Father" (John 6:65).

REMARKS: When Jesus said, "I am the way, and the truth, and the life. No one comes to the Father except through me," (John 14:6) he was making a strong affirmation that he alone was the only way to heaven. Only those who have heard the gospel message can be saved. It is an unfortunate reality that some people have been lost never having heard about Jesus Christ. Nevertheless, the important element to remember is that the call to salvation is wholly of grace, and no one has the right to demand that grace.

11

Justification

ANSWER: God does not infuse righteousness into sinners but pardons their sins and accounts their persons as righteous in Jesus Christ. *(a)* *(b)* God imputes to sinners Christ's obedience unto the whole law and his obedience unto death. *(c)*

(a) And to the one who does not work but believes in him who justifies the ungodly, his faith is counted as righteousness, just as David also speaks of the blessing of the one to whom God counts righteousness apart from works: "Blessed are those whose lawless deeds are forgiven, and whose sins are covered; blessed is the man against whom the Lord will not count his sin" (Rom 4:5–8).

(b) In him we have redemption through his blood, the forgiveness of our trespasses, according to the riches of his grace (Eph 1:7).

(c) Indeed, I count everything as loss because of the surpassing worth of knowing Christ Jesus my Lord. For his sake I have suffered the loss of all things and count them as rubbish, in order that I may gain Christ and be found in him, not having a righteousness of my own that comes from the law, but that which comes through faith in Christ, the righteousness from God that depends on faith (Phil 3:8–9).

REMARKS: Martin Luther considered justification the article upon which the church stands or falls. So important is the doctrine of justification that it proved to be the theological fault line that divided Roman Catholics from Protestants. Broadly speaking, the former distinguishes between initial justification—administered through baptism—and final justification, accomplished only after having fulfilled certain preconditions. Standing in stark contrast is the Protestant belief in the singular and judicial act by God whereby he legally declares individuals righteous because of the work of Jesus.

QUESTION 11–2: WHAT IS THE INSTRUMENT GOD USES TO JUSTIFY THE SOUL?

ANSWER: Faith receiving and resting on Christ and His righteousness is the sole instrument of justification. *(a)*

(a) For we hold that one is justified by faith apart from works of the law (Rom 3:28).

REMARKS: Saving faith is more than an intellectual assent. Christianity does not teach easy–believism. Anyone who makes this charge does understand what is meant by salvation by faith alone. Genuine faith involves three basic steps: a comprehension of the gospel message, agreement with what the Bible says about salvation, and committing one's self to God.

QUESTION 11–3: FOR WHOM DID CHRIST DIE?

ANSWER: Christ was obedient unto death, and by so doing fully dismissed the debt of all those who were elected to be the heirs of salvation. *(a) (b)*

(a) For by a single offering he has perfected for all time those who are being sanctified (Heb 10:14).

(b) But he was wounded for our transgressions; he was crushed for our iniquities; upon him was the chastisement that brought us peace, and with his stripes we are healed. All we like sheep have gone astray; we have turned—every one—to his own way; and the LORD has laid on him the iniquity of us all (Isa 53:5–6).

REMARKS: The Bible teaches that Christ died for those whom the Father gave Him (Matt 26:28; John 17:9). This was first proclaimed by the angels when they declared that Jesus had come to save his people from their sins (Matt 1:21). The atoning work of Christ was not designed to make men savable but to purchase their salvation with his own blood (1 Pet. 1:19). While the work of the cross was sufficient to save all of mankind, it was not designed to do so.

QUESTION 11-4: DOES ELECTION SAVE?

ANSWER: Even though God decreed to justify all the elect from eternity, *(a) (b) (c)* sinners are not justified personally until the Holy Spirit applies Christ to them. *(d) (e)*

(a) Even as he chose us in him before the foundation of the world, that we should be holy and blameless before him. In love he predestined us for adoption as sons through Jesus Christ, according to the purpose of his will (Eph 1:4–6).

(b) And the Scripture, foreseeing that God would justify the Gentiles by faith, preached the gospel beforehand to Abraham, saying, "In you shall all the nations be blessed" (Gal 3:8).

(c) According to the foreknowledge of God the Father, in the sanctification of the Spirit, for obedience to Jesus Christ and for sprinkling with his blood (1 Pet 1:2).

(d) And you, who once were alienated and hostile in mind, doing evil deeds, he has now reconciled in his body of flesh by his death, in order to present you holy and blameless and above reproach before him (Col 1:21–22).

(e) But when the goodness and loving kindness of God our Savior appeared, he saved us, not because of works done by us in righteousness, but according to his own mercy, by the washing of regeneration and renewal of the Holy Spirit, whom he poured out on us richly through Jesus Christ our Savior, so that being justified by his grace we might become heirs according to the hope of eternal life (Titus 3:4–7).

REMARKS: Opponents of election often insist that God foresaw who would have faith in him and elected them based upon that knowledge. But nowhere in the text of Scripture can we find this concept. What is in the bible is the teaching that predestination and election are based upon God's love and good pleasure (Eph 1:5, 10; Deut 7:7–8).

QUESTION 11–5: CAN A PERSON LOSE HIS JUSTIFICATION?

ANSWER: God continues to forgive the sins of those that are justified. *(a)* The saved individual can never fall from a state of justification, *(b)* but can fall under God's displeasure by his own sins until he repents. *(c)*

(a) But if we walk in the light, as he is in the light, we have fellowship with one another, and the blood of Jesus his Son cleanses us from all sin. If we say we have no sin, we deceive ourselves, and the truth is not in us. If we confess our sins, he is faithful and just to forgive us our sins and to cleanse us from all unrighteousness (1 John 1:7–9).

(b) I give them eternal life, and they will never perish, and no one will snatch them out of my hand (John 10:28).

(c) If they violate my statutes and do not keep my commandments, then I will punish their transgression with the rod and their iniquity with stripes, but I will not remove from him my steadfast love or be false to my faithfulness (Ps 89:31–33).

REMARKS: The words of John should give every Christian hope and comfort in knowing that the Lord gives eternal life "and they shall never perish, and no one will snatch them out of my hand" (John 10:28). He protects his chosen people from the snares of the devil. The general warnings in Scripture concerning apostasy were not written to cast doubt on the doctrine of perseverance, but were intended to serve as a warning against arrogant presumption and careless living.

QUESTION 11–6: HOW WERE BELIEVERS IN THE OLD TESTAMENT ERA JUSTIFIED?

ANSWER: The justification of believers under the Old Testament was the same as those who were justified under the New Testament. *(a)* *(b)*

(a) So then, those who are of faith are blessed along with Abraham, the man of faith (Gal 3:9).

(b) That is why his faith was "counted to him as righteousness." But the words 'it was counted to him' were not written for his sake alone, but for ours also. It will be counted to us who believe in him who raised from the dead Jesus our Lord (Rom 4:22–24).

REMARKS: Classical Dispensationalism is a theological concept that separates law and grace. It teaches that there have been two groups of men with whom the Lord has entered into a relationship. These two groups have two different purposes, one heavenly the other earthly, and have been redeemed in two distinct manners. This is contrasted with Covenant Theology, which teaches that God has always had one people with one purpose and one path towards salvation—through faith alone.

12

Adoption

QUESTION 12-1: WHAT GIFT ACCOMPANIES JUSTIFICATION?

ANSWER: All those that are justified are adopted as children through Jesus Christ, *(a) (b)* and they shall enjoy the liberties and privileges as children of God. *(c)*

(a) He predestined us for adoption as sons through Jesus Christ, according to the purpose of his will (Eph 1:5).

(b) But when the fullness of time had come, God sent forth his Son, born of woman, born under the law, to redeem those who were under the law, so that we might receive adoption as sons (Gal 4:4–5).

(c) But to all who did receive him, who believed in his name, he gave the right to become children of God (John 1:12).

REMARKS: There is a widespread misunderstanding in Christendom today that all people are children of God. Jesus rejected this concept when he told a Jewish crowd, "If God were your Father, you would love me, for I came from God and I am here. I came not of my own accord, but he sent me. Why do you not understand what I say? It is because you cannot bear to hear my word. You are of your father the devil, and your will is to do your father's desires" (John 8:42–44). One must first be saved before he is adopted into the family of God. And once we have become children of God we achieve the crowning blessing and become fellow heirs with Christ (Rom 8:17).

QUESTION 12–2: WHAT HAPPENS WHEN WE ARE ADOPTED AND BECOME CHILDREN OF GOD?

ANSWER: When we are adopted we have access to the throne of grace and are protected, *(a)* provided for, *(b)* and disciplined by him as by a Father, *(c)* yet are never forsaken, *(d) (e)* but kept for the day of redemption. *(f)*

(a) In the fear of the LORD one has strong confidence, and his children will have a refuge (Prov 14:26).

(b) Casting all your anxieties on him, because he cares for you (1 Pet 5:7).

(c) For the Lord disciplines the one he loves, and chastises every son whom he receives (Heb 12:6).

(d) "In overflowing anger for a moment I hid my face from you, but with everlasting love I will have compassion on you," says the LORD, your Redeemer. "This is like the days of Noah to me: as I swore that the waters of Noah should no more go over the earth, so I have sworn that I will not be angry with you, and will not rebuke you" (Isa 54:8–9).

(e) For the Lord will not cast off forever (Lam 3:31).

(f) And do not grieve the Holy Spirit of God, by whom you were sealed for the day of redemption (Eph 4:30).

REMARKS: Adoption must be understood properly from regeneration. The latter is a change of our moral nature while adoption is a change in our relationship with God. If you have children you know that they have a special relationship with you that your neighbor's children do not have. Likewise, when we become children of God we occupy a special standing with our heavenly Father. Our adopted status as God's children means that God loves us—in and through Jesus Christ—and that we will share the glory that is Christ's.

13

Sanctification

QUESTION 13-1: WHAT HAPPENS IN THE PROCESS OF SANCTIFICATION?

ANSWER: Through the ministry of the Word and Spirit dwelling in the believer, *(a) (b)* the power of the whole body of sin is destroyed *(c)* and the lustful desires are further weakened and put to death *(d)* as the believer becomes more Christ-like by the practice of all true holiness.

(a) Sanctify them in the truth; your word is truth (John 17:17).

(b) That according to the riches of his glory he may grant you to be strengthened with power through his Spirit in your inner being, so that Christ may dwell in your hearts through faith—that you, being rooted and grounded in love, may have strength to comprehend with all the saints what is the breadth and length and height and depth, and to know the love of Christ that surpasses knowledge, that you may be filled with all the fullness of God (Eph 3:16–19).

(c) For sin will have no dominion over you, since you are not under law but under grace (Rom 6:14).

(d) And those who belong to Christ Jesus have crucified the flesh with its passions and desires (Gal 5:24).

REMARKS: The moment we are justified we are made right with the Lord, but his grace is not exhausted at that point. The process of becoming more Christ-like is immediate with the help of the Holy Spirit. This process helps us to be freed from the bondage of tyranny and sin. Each regenerated individual experiences sanctification differently.

Some are released from the sins of their past immediately while others struggle mightily and grow slowly. Regardless of how we mature in Christ, we will never be completely free from the power of sin until we are in heaven (Heb 12:23; Rev 14:5).

QUESTION 13-2: WHAT TYPE OF SPIRITUAL WARFARE EXISTS IN A CHRISTIAN?

ANSWER: Man remains imperfect in this life and still contains some remnants of corruption in every part. *(a) (b)*

> *(a)* For I know that nothing good dwells in me, that is, in my flesh. For I have the desire to do what is right, but not the ability to carry it out (Rom 7:18).

> *(b)* But I see in my members another law waging war against the law of my mind and making me captive to the law of sin that dwells in my members (Rom 7:23).

REMARKS: Being more Christ-like is not an easy task. We need the gift of the Holy Spirit working in us to help us put off our old lives and to put on new ones in Christ. Paul outlines six examples that Christians must turn from once they are saved. Specifically: turn from lying (Eph 4:25), turn from anger (v. 26), turn from stealing (v. 28), turn from vile speech (v. 29), turn from bitterness, wrath, and malice (v. 30), and turn from sexual sins (Eph 5:3). Here we are warned that no one who practices these sins will inherit the kingdom of God.

QUESTION 13-3: IS THERE HOPE FOR THE BELIEVER'S SANCTIFICATION IN THE STRUGGLE FOR HOLINESS?

ANSWER: Although the remaining corruption may prevail for a time, *(a)* the strength from the Holy Spirit will help overcome sin *(b)* and help the saints grow in grace. *(c) (d)*

> *(a)* But I see in my members another law waging war against the law of my mind and making me captive to the law of sin that dwells in my members (Rom 7:23).

> *(b)* For sin will have no dominion over you, since you are not under law but under grace (Rom 6:14).

(c) Rather, speaking the truth in love, we are to grow up in every way into him who is the head, into Christ (Eph 4:15).

(d) And we all, with unveiled face, beholding the glory of the Lord, are being transformed into the same image from one degree of glory to another. For this comes from the Lord who is the Spirit (2 Cor 3:18).

REMARKS: There are practical steps believers can take in their quest to be conformed more so to the image of Christ. They are not to sit casually by and wait for extraordinary measures to happen mysteriously. Christians are commanded to live out their lives by "making their calling and election sure" (2 Pet 1:10). We accomplish this by having faith, studying the word of God, partaking of the ordinances, praying and fellowshipping with other Christians, and receiving divine discipline from the Father. Each of these means serve to sanctify believers and to carry them along the path towards their pursuit of holiness.

14

Faith

QUESTION 14–1: WHAT IS SAVING FAITH?

ANSWER: The grace of faith is the enabling to believe to the saving of the soul brought by the work of the Holy Spirit in the heart. *(a) (b)*

> *(a)* Since we have the same spirit of faith according to what has been written, "I believed, and so I spoke," we also believe, and so we also speak (2 Cor 4:13).

> *(b)* For by grace you have been saved through faith. And this is not your own doing; it is the gift of God (Eph 2:8).

REMARKS: One of the tenants of the Protestant Reformation was the belief that faith alone is the means or instrument by which a person is saved. Christians are justified by faith, and it is through that faith they continue to live their lives to glorify God and sustain their hope of something better to come.

QUESTION 14–2: HOW IS SAVING FAITH INCREASED AND STRENGTHENED?

ANSWER: Faith is ordinarily brought by preaching the Word *(a) (b)* and is increased and strengthened by the administration of baptism, the Lord's Supper, and through prayer. *(c) (d) (e)*

> *(a)* How then will they call on him in whom they have not believed? And how are they to believe in him of whom they have never heard? And how are they to hear without someone preaching (Rom 10:14)?

> *(b)* So faith comes from hearing, and hearing through the word of Christ (Rom 10:17).

(c) The apostles said to the Lord, "Increase our faith" (Luke 17:5)!

(d) Like newborn infants, long for the pure spiritual milk, that by it you may grow up into salvation (1 Pet 2:2).

(e) And now I commend you to God and to the word of his grace, which is able to build you up and to give you the inheritance among all those who are sanctified (Acts 20:32).

REMARKS: Strength training requires constant repetitions through incremental weight additions in order to increase in strength. Similarly, the Christian's spiritual growth will only come through diligent work and intense study little by little. When the Christian applies himself to learning God's Word and fellowships with other believer's he will naturally grow in grace and truth.

QUESTION 14-3: WHAT ARE THE EXPRESSIONS OF TRUE FAITH?

ANSWER: By faith a Christian believes the Word of God, *(a)* embraces the person and work of Jesus Christ, is obedient to the gospel message, *(b)* trembles at the warnings of judgment to come, *(c)* embraces the promises of God for this life and that which is to come, *(d)* and accepts Jesus Christ alone as the means of salvation. *(e) (f)*

(a) But this I confess to you, that according to the Way, which they call a sect, I worship the God of our fathers, believing everything laid down by the Law and written in the Prophets (Acts 24:14).

(b) You are my friends if you do what I command you (John 15:14).

(c) All these things my hand has made, and so all these things came to be, declares the LORD. But this is the one to whom I will look: he who is humble and contrite in spirit and trembles at my word (Isa 66:2).

(d) These all died in faith, not having received the things promised, but having seen them and greeted them from afar, and having acknowledged that they were strangers and exiles on the earth (Heb 11:3).

(e) But to all who did receive him, who believed in his name, he gave the right to become children of God (John 1:12).

(f) And they said, "Believe in the Lord Jesus, and you will be saved, you and your household" (Acts 16:31).

REMARKS: The Bible differentiates between an intellectual assent of Jesus Christ and a personal trust in him. James records that even the demons believe—and shudder (Jas 2:19). Saving faith transcends a mere cognitive knowledge of Christ and is described as a personal act that involves the heart, mind, and will that is given over to the one true God.

15

Repentance and Salvation

Question 15-1: Can a person who has lived long in sin still be saved?

Answer: God can call his elect unto repentance at any point in an individual's life, even if that person has committed egregious sins, having served various lusts and pleasures. *(a)*

(a) To speak evil of no one, to avoid quarreling, to be gentle, and to show perfect courtesy toward all people. For we ourselves were once foolish, disobedient, led astray, slaves to various passions and pleasures, passing our days in malice and envy, hated by others and hating one another. But when the goodness and loving kindness of God our Savior appeared, he saved us, not because of works done by us in righteousness, but according to his own mercy, by the washing of regeneration and renewal of the Holy Spirit (Tit 3:2–5).

Remarks: There are no sins too great for God's mercy. Paul referred to himself as the chief of all sinners (1 Tim 1:15), yet he was an apostle of Christ. The important lesson to remember is that each of us has been at one time or another at enmity with God (Rom 8:7). It is only through the work of the Holy Spirit that our hearts are changed so that we can realize our desperate plight and need for God's grace.

Question 15-2: What does God grant to sinners?

Answer: God grants saving repentance, *(a) (b)* whereby a person is made aware by the Holy Spirit of his numerous sins, humbles himself with godly sorrow, and detests his wicked ways. *(c)*

(a) When they heard these things they fell silent. And they glorified God, saying, "Then to the Gentiles also God has granted repentance that leads to life" (Acts 11:18).

(b) And I will pour out on the house of David and the inhabitants of Jerusalem a spirit of grace and pleas for mercy, so that, when they look on me, on him whom they have pierced, they shall mourn for him, as one mourns for an only child, and weep bitterly over him, as one weeps over a firstborn (Zech 12:10).

(c) Then you will remember your evil ways, and your deeds that were not good, and you will loathe yourselves for your iniquities and your abominations (Ezek 36:31).

REMARKS: Repentance means a fundamental change in a person so that every facet of his life is altered for the better. It is starting life anew. When a sinner repents, he does something more than intellectually acknowledges that he is sinning against God—he changes. But he does not repent because he has some superior knowledge or is godlier than his unrepentant neighbor. Rather, his repentance is the fruit of regeneration. Also accompanying repentance is faith. Turning away from sin and to Christ is impossible without saving faith. We are not saved because we repented and have faith, but rather, we repented and have faith because we are saved.

QUESTION 15–3: ARE WE REQUIRED TO REPENT OF OUR SINS AFTER WE HAVE BEEN SAVED?

ANSWER: Repentance is to be continued through the course of our lives. It is every one's duty to repent of known sins. (a) (b)

(a) And Zacchaeus stood and said to the Lord, "Behold, Lord, the half of my goods I give to the poor. And if I have defrauded anyone of anything, I restore it fourfold" (Luke 19:8).

(b) Though formerly I was a blasphemer, persecutor, and insolent opponent. But I received mercy because I had acted ignorantly in unbelief, and the grace of our Lord overflowed for me with the faith and love that are in Christ Jesus. The saying is trustworthy and deserving of full acceptance, that Christ Jesus came into the world to save sinners, of whom I am the foremost (1 Tim 1:13–15).

REMARKS: David provides for us an example of true repentance (Ps 51). In his lament, he expresses more than remorse, self-hatred, and anguish for getting caught. Instead, he expresses genuine sorrow for sinning against God (v. 4). He displays the true intent of his heart in that he turned away from his iniquities and lived a righteous life.

QUESTION 15–4: IS THERE A SIN TOO GREAT FOR THE GRACE OF GOD?

ANSWER: There is no sin that shall bring damnation on them that repent. *(a) (b)*

> *(a)* For the wages of sin is death, but the free gift of God is eternal life in Christ Jesus our Lord (Rom 6:23).

> *(b)* Let the wicked forsake his way, and the unrighteous man his thoughts; let him return to the LORD, that he may have compassion on him, and to our God, for he will abundantly pardon (Isa 55:7).

REMARKS: The Bible teaches there is one sin that will never be forgiven either in this world or the next. This is referred to as "the unpardonable sin." The Gospels of Matthew, Mark, and Luke each qualify this sin as blasphemy against the Holy Spirit (Matt 12:31–32; Mark 3:28–30; Luke 12:10). There were some followers in the days of Jesus that were saying his power to do good did not come from God but was granted from the devil. This unpardonable sin is different from other sins in that it directly assaults the Holy Spirit. It is the Spirit's work to quicken sinners and give them the ability and desire to repent. But when this is freely rejected, the Lord leaves the sinner in his state and permits him to dwell in his own sin to his eternal destruction.

16

Good Works

QUESTION 16–1: WHAT CONSTITUTES A GOOD WORK?

ANSWER: Good works are only those actions God has commanded in his Word. *(a) (b)*

(a) He has told you, O man, what is good; and what does the LORD require of you but to do justice, and to love kindness, and to walk humbly with your God (Mic 6:8)?

(b) Equip you with everything good that you may do his will, working in us that which is pleasing in his sight, through Jesus Christ, to whom be glory forever and ever. Amen (Heb 13:21).

REMARKS: Many atheists have tried to argue that good works can exist outside of a Lawgiver. They point to their own lives as proof that they are thoughtful and caring individuals—similar to their Christian neighbors—yet they are free not to believe in God. The problem with this conviction is that the apostle Paul tells us everything that does not proceed from faith is sin (Rom 14:23). If an individual does not act from the inner conviction of the Holy Spirit it is the result of selfish motives and is sinful. Moreover, what man sees as good works are merely "polluted garments" to a holy God (Isa 64:6).

QUESTION 16–2: WHAT IS THE PURPOSE OF GOOD WORKS?

ANSWER: Good works done in obedience to God's commandments are the fruits and evidences of a true and living faith. *(a) (b)*

(a) And by this we know that we have come to know him, if we keep his commandments (1 John 2:3).

(b) But whoever keeps his word, in him truly the love of God is perfected. By this we may know that we are in him (1 John 2:5).

REMARKS: Sinners are justified by faith, but justifying faith is not alone. Christians have been saved unto good works, but there are many that falsely assume they do not have to perform good works or to keep the law since they are in Christ. Those who hold to this persuasion are called Antinomians, which means "against the law." It is inconsistent with the gospel message to have true saving faith and not to have the desire to obey God by keeping his commands. Any one who is a new creature will perform good works as an expression of his genuine conversion.

QUESTION 16–3: WHAT IS THE RELATIONSHIP BETWEEN HUMAN RESPONSIBILITY AND DIVINE ENABLING?

ANSWER: The ability to perform good works is given by the Holy Spirit. *(a)* Nevertheless, the believer must be diligent in stirring up the grace of God that is in him. *(b)*

(a) Abide in me, and I in you. As the branch cannot bear fruit by itself, unless it abides in the vine, neither can you, unless you abide in me. I am the vine; you are the branches. Whoever abides in me and I in him, he it is that bears much fruit, for apart from me you can do nothing (John 15:4–5).

(b) Therefore, my beloved, as you have always obeyed, so now, not only as in my presence but much more in my absence, work out your own salvation with fear and trembling (Phil 2:12).

REMARKS: The Bible uses the metaphor of a vine to illustrate the relationship between God and man. God is the vine that supplies nutrients to the branches in order that they might bear fruit. This picture should serve to remind us that we can only perform good works when the Holy Spirit enables us to do so.

QUESTION 16–4: CAN CHRISTIAN SAINTS GATHER UP GOOD WORKS SO AS TO APPLY THEM TO OTHERS?

ANSWER: Those who in their obedience attain to the greatest height which is possible in this life and are able to do more than God requires still fall short of their duty to which they are bound. *(a) (b)*

   (a) "Truly I know that it is so: But how can a man be in the right before God? If one wished to contend with him, one could not answer him once in a thousand times" (Job 9:2–3).

   (b) So you also, when you have done all that you were commanded, say, "We are unworthy servants; we have only done what was our duty" (Luke 17:10).

REMARKS: The treasury of merit is a concept that developed within the Roman Catholic Church long after the Apostles. This was the idea that Christ and the saints have stored up excessive merit which goes into the treasury and is available to the Church to distribute as she sees fit. Any withdrawal of merit from the treasury comes in the form of an indulgence, which is used to forgive sin and to be reconciled with God. Those who oppose this doctrine appeal to Scripture which speaks of only one way to be reconciled with the Father—through his Son, Jesus Christ (Rom 5:10–12).

QUESTION 16–5: CAN ANYONE MERIT ETERNAL SALVATION?

ANSWER: Even our best works cannot merit pardon of sin or eternal life because of the great divide that separates us from God. The gift of God cannot be earned or merited. *(a) (b) (c)*

   (a) For by works of the law no human being will be justified in his sight, since through the law comes knowledge of sin (Rom 3:20).

   (b) For by grace you have been saved through faith. And this is not your own doing; it is the gift of God, not a result of works, so that no one may boast (Eph 2:8–9).

   (c) Just as David also speaks of the blessing of the one to whom God counts righteousness apart from works (Rom 4:6).

REMARKS: Anyone who believes that the work of Jesus Christ, in and of itself, is not sufficient to save anyone apart from human works believes in a works–based salvation. That is, anyone who adds anything to the work of Jesus on the cross (whether sacraments, good works performed in a state of grace, or whatever) is guilty of adding to the biblical teaching of justification by grace through faith alone (Eph 2:8–9). Man can no more merit his own salvation through good works than a leopard can change his spots (Jer 13:23). To say otherwise is to misunderstand the condition of fallen man. Only after the Spirit has set the will free can it choose righteousness freely.

QUESTION 16–6: WHAT IS THE BASIS FOR WHICH OUR GOOD WORKS ARE ACCEPTABLE TO GOD?

ANSWER: The works of men are never acceptable to God. *(a)* However, as an expression of gospel obedience and on the basis of the finished work of Christ, good works are pleasing to the Father. *(b) (c) (d)*

(a) We have all become like one who is unclean, and all our righteous deeds are like a polluted garment. We all fade like a leaf, and our iniquities, like the wind, take us away (Isa 64:6).

(b) You yourselves like living stones are being built up as a spiritual house, to be a holy priesthood, to offer spiritual sacrifices acceptable to God through Jesus Christ (1 Pet 2:5).

(c) His master said to him, "Well done, good and faithful servant. You have been faithful over a little; I will set you over much. Enter into the joy of your master" (Matt 25:21).

(d) For God is not unjust so as to overlook your work and the love that you have shown for his name in serving the saints, as you still do (Heb 6:10).

REMARKS: The constant cycle of animal sacrifices in the Old Testament served as a reminder to the Israelites that they had sinned against a holy God. It was to remind them that their sin had consequences, but it also pointed to something greater yet to come. The New Testament believer did not have this remembrance because Jesus Christ came as the perfect sacrifice to take away the sin of the world once and for all. Because of his obedience unto death, God forgives the sins of believers and remembers their iniquities no more (Jer 31:34). When God looks upon his chosen people he sees them cloaked in the righteousness of Jesus Christ.

QUESTION 16-7: CAN THE UNREGENERATE PERFORM GOOD WORKS THAT ARE PLEASING TO GOD?

ANSWER: Works performed by unregenerate men are sinful and cannot please God *(a) (b)* because they do not proceed from a heart purified by faith, *(c) (d)* nor are they done in a right manner according to Scripture, *(e)* or for the glory of God. *(f) (g)*

(a) I hate, I despise your feasts, and I take no delight in your solemn assemblies. Even though you offer me your burnt offerings and grain offerings, I will not accept them; and the peace offerings of your fattened animals, I will not look upon them (Amos 5:21–22).

(b) So then it depends not on human will or exertion, but on God, who has mercy (Rom 9:16).

(c) By faith Abel offered to God a more acceptable sacrifice than Cain, through which he was commended as righteous, God commending him by accepting his gifts. And through his faith, though he died, he still speaks (Heb 11:4).

(d) And without faith it is impossible to please him, for whoever would draw near to God must believe that he exists and that he rewards those who seek him (Heb 11:6).

(e) If I speak in the tongues of men and of angels, but have not love, I am a noisy gong or a clanging cymbal (1 Cor 13:1).

(f) Thus, when you give to the needy, sound no trumpet before you, as the hypocrites do in the synagogues and in the streets, that they may be praised by others. Truly, I say to you, they have received their reward (Matt 6:2).

(g) "And when you pray, you must not be like the hypocrites. For they love to stand and pray in the synagogues and at the street corners, that they may be seen by others. Truly, I say to you, they have received their reward" (Matt 6:5).

REMARKS: The offerings of Cain and Abel offer a vivid account of the principle that sacrifices without faith are worthless. From the beginning of the Old Testament, faith has been absolutely necessary in order to please God or to worship him properly.

17

Perseverance

QUESTION 17-1: WHAT DOES IT MEANS WHEN ONE SPEAKS OF THE PERSEVERANCE OF THE SAINTS?

ANSWER: Those whom God called and sanctified by his Spirit can neither totally nor finally fall from a state of salvation, but will certainly be preserved to the end. *(a) (b) (c)*

(a) I give them eternal life, and they will never perish, and no one will snatch them out of my hand. My Father, who has given them to me, is greater than all, and no one is able to snatch them out of the Father's hand (John 10:28–29).

(b) And I am sure of this, that he who began a good work in you will bring it to completion at the day of Jesus Christ (Phil 1:6).

(c) They went out from us, but they were not of us; for if they had been of us, they would have continued with us. But they went out, that it might become plain that they all are not of us (1 John 2:19).

REMARKS: The perseverance of the saints might be understood in clearer terms if we define what is meant by the phrase. Perseverance means continued adherence to the Christian belief despite battling opposition and discouragement. But it is not the strength of the Christian alone that ensures he will persevere unto the end. Christ assures us that none who are his will be lost and promises that each will be glorified at the last day (John 6:39). To put it another way, we persevere because we are being preserved.

QUESTION 17-2: DOES PERSEVERANCE MEAN THAT CHRISTIANS WILL NEVER COMMIT EGREGIOUS SIN?

ANSWER: Christians will inevitably encounter formidable trials and temptations, yet they shall never be removed from the foundation of Jesus Christ. Nevertheless, sin can temporarily cause the sight of the light and love of God to be clouded and obscured from Christians. *(a) (b)*

> *(a)* If they violate my statutes and do not keep my commandments, then I will punish their transgression with the rod and their iniquity with stripes (Ps 89:31–32).

> *(b)* But when we are judged by the Lord, we are disciplined so that we may not be condemned along with the world (1 Cor 11:32).

REMARKS: The doctrine of perseverance is oftentimes caricatured by opponents who insist that this view allows for Christians to live as wickedly as they want and still be saved. This, however, is a misunderstanding of the doctrine and what it teaches. When properly understood, perseverance does not lead to living carelessly and arrogant presumption. The saved individual will repudiated his former vices because he has been given a new nature. Even though he may backslide and fall into sin, the Holy Spirit will convict him and grant him the desire to repent (John 16:8).

QUESTION 17-3: WHAT CONFIDENCE DO WE HAVE OF PERSEVERANCE?

ANSWER: Christians have confidence in the power of God unto salvation *(a)* and through faith in Christ Jesus to the end. *(b)*

> *(a)* For I the LORD do not change; therefore you, O children of Jacob, are not consumed (Mal 3:6).

> *(b)* But I have prayed for you that your faith may not fail. And when you have turned again, strengthen your brothers (Luke 22:32).

REMARKS: John tells us that Jesus Christ entered into a covenant with his Father (John 6:37–40) to keep his people from being lost (John 10:28). Jesus asked his Father to preserve those whom he was given, and it is inconceivable to think God would not honor his request. Our confidence does not rest in our own ability to perform good works but solely in Christ who continues to intercede on our behalf.

18

Assurance of Grace

QUESTION 18–1: IS THERE A FALSE SALVATION?

ANSWER: Temporary believers and other unregenerate men may deceive themselves with false hopes and carnal presumptions of being in the favor of God and in a state of salvation, which hope of theirs shall perish. *(a) (b)*

(a) Such are the paths of all who forget God; the hope of the godless shall perish. His confidence is severed, and his trust is a spider's web (Job 8:13–14).

(b) On that day many will say to me, "Lord, Lord, did we not prophesy in your name, and cast out demons in your name, and do many mighty works in your name?" And then will I declare to them, "I never knew you; depart from me, you workers of lawlessness" (Matt 7:22–23).

REMARKS: Jesus warned his followers to be on guard for false prophets who preached one thing yet lived differently. The same is true for individuals who profess the name of Christ but live according to the world. It will not always be clear who are among the elect, but there will be evidence of fruit to demonstrate if an individual is reliable or untrustworthy. So, we should examine our neighbors and ourselves to ensure that we are doers of the Word and not merely sayers.

QUESTION 18–2: CAN THE BELIEVER BE ASSURED THAT HE IS IN A STATE OF GRACE?

ANSWER: The believer may be certainly assured that he is in a state of grace and may rejoice in the hope of the glory of God *(a) (b) (c) (d)* which hope shall never make him ashamed. *(e)*

> *(a)* And by this we know that we have come to know him, if we keep his commandments (1 John 2:3).

> *(b)* Little children, let us not love in word or talk but in deed and in truth. By this we shall know that we are of the truth and reassure our heart before him; for whenever our heart condemns us, God is greater than our heart, and he knows everything. Beloved, if our heart does not condemn us, we have confidence before God (1 John 3:18–21).

> *(c)* I write these things to you who believe in the name of the Son of God that you may know that you have eternal life (1 John 5:13).

> *(d)* Through him we have also obtained access by faith into this grace in which we stand, and we rejoice in hope of the glory of God (Rom 5:2).

> *(e)* And hope does not put us to shame, because God's love has been poured into our hearts through the Holy Spirit who has been given to us (Rom 5:5).

REMARKS: The New Testament speaks of hope as being the assurance of something not yet experienced. Our hope is not based on uncertain, wishful thinking but on Jesus Christ who is called "our hope" (1 Tim 1:1). This world is rife with trials and tribulations, but the Lord will give us strength to fight the good fight until he returns for all who believe.

QUESTION 18–3: WHAT IS THE BASIS OF THE BELIEVER'S ASSURANCE?

ANSWER: The believer's certainty is not a matter of conjecture and probable persuasion grounded upon a fallible hope, but an infallible assurance of faith *(a) (b)* founded on the blood and righteousness of Jesus Christ revealed in the Gospel. *(c)*

(a) And we desire each one of you to show the same earnestness to have the full assurance of hope until the end (Heb 6:11).

(b) We have this as a sure and steadfast anchor of the soul, a hope that enters into the inner place behind the curtain (Heb 6:19).

(c) So when God desired to show more convincingly to the heirs of the promise the unchangeable character of his purpose, he guaranteed it with an oath, so that by two unchangeable things, in which it is impossible for God to lie, we who have fled for refuge might have strong encouragement to hold fast to the hope set before us (Heb 6:17–18).

REMARKS: The Christian can take comfort in knowing that the God who has chosen him from the foundation of the world (Eph 1:4) will reside eternally in his sovereign care. There is a divine certainty the elect will be brought to dwell with the Lord in heaven (John 14:1–4; Rom 8:28–29; Phil 1:6). Christ assures his own they will not be lost but will be glorified at the last day (John 6:39). To put it another way, what Christ has promised he will perform.

QUESTION 18–4: CAN A BELIEVER FALL INTO SIN?

ANSWER: Even though God may withdraw the light of his face, the believer is never destitute of the seed of God (a) and life of faith, (b) because by the operation of the Spirit, the believer will be revived (c) and preserved from utter despair. (d)

(a) No one born of God makes a practice of sinning, for God's seed abides in him, and he cannot keep on sinning because he has been born of God (1 John 3:9).

(b) "But I have prayed for you that your faith may not fail. And when you have turned again, strengthen your brothers" (Luke 22:32).

(c) Why are you cast down, O my soul, and why are you in turmoil within me? Hope in God; for I shall again praise him, my salvation (Ps 42:5).

(d) It is good that one should wait quietly for the salvation of the LORD. It is good for a man that he bear the yoke in his youth. Let him sit alone in silence when it is laid on him; let him put his mouth in the dust—there may yet be hope; let him give his cheek to the one who strikes, and let him be filled with insults. For the Lord will not cast off forever (Lam 3:26–31).

REMARKS: Sin clouds our minds and impairs our judgement so that we resist what the Scripture commands us to do. The Lord sometimes allows us to dwell in our sin for a season in order to teach us spiritual lessons. But if we are truly children of God, the Holy Spirit will work within us to enlighten us so that we will eventually see the wickedness of our ways and the hardness of our hearts and compel us to repent of our sins. God guarantees final future deliverance from sin and eternal life in heaven (1 Pet 1:8).

19

The Law of God

QUESTION 19-1: WHAT AGREEMENT DID GOD MAKE WITH
THE FIRST MAN AND ALL HIS POSTERITY?

ANSWER: God gave to Adam a law of universal obedience written on
his heart, and a command not to eat the fruit of the tree of knowledge
of good and evil. *(a)* God bound Adam and all his descendents to
absolute obedience, *(b)* whereby he was promised life upon fulfilling
the law and threatened with death upon breaking it. *(c)*

  (a) But God said, "You shall not eat of the fruit of the tree that is in
  the midst of the garden, neither shall you touch it, lest you die"
  (Gen 3:3).

  (b) For Moses writes about the righteousness that is based on the
  law, that the person who does the commandments shall live by
  them (Rom 10:5).

  (c) For all who rely on works of the law are under a curse; for it is
  written, "Cursed be everyone who does not abide by all things
  written in the Book of the Law, and do them." Now it is evident
  that no one is justified before God by the law, for "The righteous
  shall live by faith." But the law is not of faith, rather "The one
  who does them shall live by them" (Gal 3:10–12).

REMARKS: God did not create mankind autonomous but theonomous,
that is, subject to his authority. God gave man everything he could
have imagined but placed upon him only one prohibition—not to eat
of the tree of the knowledge of good and evil (Gen 3:3). The temptation eventually proved to be too great, and our first parents let the serpent convince them that God's motives were impure. They ultimately

yielded to their desires to be like God, and by so doing broke their covenant with their Creator.

QUESTION 19-2: IS THE AGREEMENT THAT GOD MADE WITH ADAM STILL BINDING UPON ALL MEN?

ANSWER: The same law that was first written in the heart of Adam continued to be a perfect rule of righteousness after the fall. *(a)*

(a) For when Gentiles, who do not have the law, by nature do what the law requires, they are a law to themselves, even though they do not have the law. They show that the work of the law is written on their hearts, while their conscience also bears witness, and their conflicting thoughts accuse or even excuse them (Rom 2:14–15).

REMARKS: Some had tried to argue that Gentiles were excused from punishment since they did not have the faintest notion about God's law. Paul, however, addresses this objection in his epistle to the Romans in which he declared that everyone has the law of God written on the heart, leaving man without excuse (Rom 2:15). God equips everybody with a sense of right and wrong, but many exchange the truth about him for a lie.

QUESTION 19-3: WHAT IS THE MORAL LAW?

ANSWER: The moral law was given at Mount Sinai, in the ten commandments, and written in two tables, the first four containing our duty towards God, and the other six, our duty to man. *(a)*

(a) And he wrote on the tablets, in the same writing as before, the Ten Commandments that the LORD had spoken to you on the mountain out of the midst of the fire on the day of the assembly. And the LORD gave them to me (Deut 10:4).

REMARKS: John Calvin taught that the Scripture set forth three functions for the laws of God: to serve as a mirror to reflect the perfect righteousness of God on us to reveal our own shortcomings; to serve as a restraint against lawlessness and evil; and to serve as a guide to exhort believers unto good works.

QUESTION 19-4: WHAT OTHER LAWS DID GOD GIVE TO ISRAEL?

ANSWER: In addition to the moral law, God gave the people of Israel ceremonial laws containing several typical ordinances anticipating the person and work of Jesus Christ. *(a) (b)*

(a) For since the law has but a shadow of the good things to come instead of the true form of these realities, it can never, by the same sacrifices that are continually offered every year, make perfect those who draw near (Heb 10:1).

(b) These are a shadow of the things to come, but the substance belongs to Christ (Col 2:17).

REMARKS: The Old Testament ceremonial laws were given to Israel for a temporary basis until their symbolic meaning had been fulfilled by the New Testament. Much of the books of Exodus, Leviticus, Numbers, and Deuteronomy describe in great detail the ceremonial laws that included circumcision, sacrifices, offerings, purification, holy days, and other rites of Jewish worship.

QUESTION 19-5: WHAT IS THE PURPOSE AND USAGE OF THE MORAL LAW WITHIN THE CHURCH?

ANSWER: The moral law is binding upon believers as an expression of gospel obedience. Christ did not dissolve the moral law but strengthened it. *(a) (b) (c)*

(a) Owe no one anything, except to love each other, for the one who loves another has fulfilled the law. For the commandments, "You shall not commit adultery, You shall not murder, You shall not steal, You shall not covet," and any other commandment, are summed up in this word: "You shall love your neighbor as yourself." Love does no wrong to a neighbor; therefore love is the fulfilling of the law (Rom 13:8–10).

(b) "Do not think that I have come to abolish the Law or the Prophets; I have not come to abolish them but to fulfill them" (Matt 5:17).

(c) Do we then overthrow the law by this faith? By no means! On the contrary, we uphold the law (Rom 3:31).

REMARKS: Believers are not under the moral law as a covenant of works or else no one would ever be saved. However, the moral law remains a rule of life, informs the believer of the will of God, exposes sin, and is designed to lead to conviction and repentance.

20

The Gospel and Grace

QUESTION 20-1: WHAT DID GOD DO ONCE THE COVENANT OF WORKS WAS BROKEN BY SIN?

ANSWER: God was pleased to give forth the promise of Christ as the means of calling the elect and giving them faith and repentance. *(a)*

> *(a)* "I will put enmity between you and the woman, and between your offspring and her offspring; he shall bruise your head, and you shall bruise his heel" (Gen 3:15).

REMARKS: God's mercy is clearly demonstrated in the Garden of Eden by his promise to deliver fallen man from the power of Satan. Three statements were made concerning Christ: he would come from the seed of Eve; his heel would be bruised, pointing to his humanity; and he will bruise his head—that is, Christ would be victorious over the devil's kingdom. Once the beast received the wound to the head, he would never be able to recover from it.

QUESTION 20-2: HOW WAS THE PROMISE OF CHRIST REVEALED?

ANSWER: The promise of Christ, and salvation by him, is revealed only by the Word of God. *(a)*

> *(a)* For in it the righteousness of God is revealed from faith for faith, as it is written, "The righteous shall live by faith" (Rom 1:17).

REMARKS: When sinners come to true faith in Christ, his life-long record of impeccable obedience is credited to their account and God justifies the sinners. This understanding is known as imputation. The doctrine of imputation should be distinguished from justification in that God considers the righteousness of Christ as belonging to everyone who comes by faith alone in Jesus Christ. It is on that basis that God declares sinners righteous.

QUESTION 20-3: WHAT WORK OF THE HOLY SPIRIT IS ESSENTIAL TO THE GOSPEL MESSAGE AND SALVATION?

ANSWER: Because men are dead in trespasses and sin they must be quickened or regenerated by the sovereign and effectual work of the Holy Spirit upon the whole soul so that a new spiritual life is produced. Without this special work of the Holy Spirit there is no other means of salvation. *(a)*

   (a) The natural person does not accept the things of the Spirit of God, for they are folly to him, and he is not able to understand them because they are spiritually discerned (1 Cor 2:14).

REMARKS: Reformed theology speaks of divine illumination in two stages. The first part comes through the hearing of the Word. This directly affects the second stage in which the Holy Spirit ministers to the sinner, ultimately conveying the effectual calling to salvation.

21

Christian Liberty

QUESTION 21-1: WHAT TEN LIBERTIES DID CHRIST PURCHASE FOR BELIEVERS UNDER THE GOSPEL?

ANSWER: Believers are now freed from the guilt of sin, the wrath of God, the demands and curse of the law, *(a)* and in their being delivered from this present evil world, *(b)* bondage to Satan, *(c)* and dominion of sin, *(d)* from the evil of afflictions, *(e)* the fear and sting of death, the victory of the grave, *(f)* and everlasting damnation. *(g)*

(a) Christ redeemed us from the curse of the law by becoming a curse for us—for it is written, "Cursed is everyone who is hanged on a tree" (Gal 3:13).

(b) Who gave himself for our sins to deliver us from the present evil age, according to the will of our God and Father (Gal 1:4).

(c) "To open their eyes, so that they may turn from darkness to light and from the power of Satan to God, that they may receive forgiveness of sins and a place among those who are sanctified by faith in me" (Acts 26:18).

(d) For God has done what the law, weakened by the flesh, could not do. By sending his own Son in the likeness of sinful flesh and for sin, he condemned sin in the flesh (Rom 8:3).

(e) And we know that for those who love God all things work together for good, for those who are called according to his purpose (Rom 8:28).

(f) When the perishable puts on the imperishable, and the mortal puts on immortality, then shall come to pass the saying that is written: "Death is swallowed up in victory. O death, where is

your victory? O death, where is your sting?" The sting of death is sin, and the power of sin is the law. But thanks be to God, who gives us the victory through our Lord Jesus Christ (1 Cor 15:54–57).

(g) When he comes on that day to be glorified in his saints, and to be marveled at among all who have believed, because our testimony to you was believed (2 Thess 1:10).

REMARKS: The mission of Christ on earth was one of humiliation. He willingly left behind the eternal glory that was his to take on the form of man to fulfill the covenant he had with God the Father from all eternity. Jesus' submission does not make him inferior in stature in any capacity. Rather, it demonstrates the indescribable love Christ has for his people in that he was willing to condescend by coming to earth, living a life of poverty and suffering, and dying on behalf of sinners so they could be freed from the tyranny of sin. Believers will spend eternity in the presence of the Lord because of Christ's obedience and humility.

QUESTION 21–2: HOW IS THE CONSCIENCE SET FREE, AND HOW MAY IT BE ENSLAVED?

ANSWER: God alone is Lord of the conscience, (a) and has left it free from the doctrines and commandments of men that are in any respect contrary to his Word or not contained in it. (b) (c) (d) The conscience can be enslaved when organized religion requires implicit faith and absolute and blind obedience. (e) (f)

(a) There is only one lawgiver and judge, he who is able to save and to destroy. But who are you to judge your neighbor (Jas 4:12)?

(b) But Peter and John answered them, "Whether it is right in the sight of God to listen to you rather than to God, you must judge" (Acts 4:19).

(c) You were bought with a price; do not become slaves of men (1 Cor 7:23).

(d) "In vain do they worship me, teaching as doctrines the commandments of men" (Matt 15:9).

(e) What then is Apollos? What is Paul? Servants through whom you believed, as the Lord assigned to each (1 Cor 3:5).

(f) Not that we lord it over your faith, but we work with you for your joy, for you stand firm in your faith (2 Cor 1:24).

REMARKS: Some Roman Catholics do not believe the Bible is materially sufficient for all the truths God has revealed to us. Revelation is found partly in Scripture and partly in oral traditions. This view is aptly termed the partim-partim view (partim being Latin for partly). Protestants who oppose this concept argue that the Bible does not support the idea of extra-biblical revelation. Another practical issue that must be resolved is for supporters of the partim–partim view to demonstrate empirically that this idea was taught during the apostolic era. If this cannot be accomplished, one must wonder how any soul was saved prior to the extra–biblical revelation. Additionally, it would also lead one to question why further revelation would even be necessary.

QUESTION 21-3: HOW MIGHT THE CONSCIENCE BE VIOLATED AND THE GOSPEL PERVERTED?

ANSWER: The conscience is perverted when known sin is willingly practiced and specific lust patterns are cherished. *(a) (b)*

(a) What shall we say then? Are we to continue in sin that grace may abound? By no means! How can we who died to sin still live in it (Rom 6:1–2)?

(b) For you were called to freedom, brothers. Only do not use your freedom as an opportunity for the flesh, but through love serve one another (Gal 5:13).

REMARKS: The apostle Paul makes the point that living in perpetual sin while claiming the name of Christ is a contradiction of the new birth. Christians are called to put to death the sins of the flesh. He further points out believers have been baptized with Christ Jesus in both death and resurrection, and that it is impossible for them to continue sinning the same way they did before salvation (Rom 6:3).

22

Religious Worship

QUESTION 22–1: WHAT DOES THE LIGHT OF NATURE REVEAL ABOUT GOD AND OUR RESPONSIBILITY TOWARD HIM?

ANSWER: The light of nature reveals that there is a God, who has lordship and sovereignty over all. He is just and good to all and is therefore to be feared, loved, praised, called upon, trusted in, and served with all the heart, soul, and mind. *(a) (b)*

> *(a)* Who would not fear you, O King of the nations? For this is your due; for among all the wise ones of the nations and in all their kingdoms there is none like you (Jer 10:7).

> *(b)* "And to love him with all the heart and with all the understanding and with all the strength, and to love one's neighbor as oneself, is much more than all whole burnt offerings and sacrifices" (Mark 12:33).

REMARKS: Many have read the familiar truth in the Reformed catechisms that state positively of man's chief goal being to glorify God. This axiom is true for everything we do. We have a personal calling to please God just as Christ did with his earthly ministry and subsequent death on the cross. It pleases God when we imitate Christ and his deeds so our focus should be to please God in whatever we do or say.

QUESTION 22–2: WHO ARE WE TO WORSHIP?

ANSWER: Religious worship is to be given to God the Father, Son, and Holy Spirit alone. *(a) (b) (c)* We are not to worship the angels, saints, or any other creatures. *(d) (e) (f)* (*a*) And he said to him, "All these I will give you, if you will fall down and worship me." Then Jesus said to him, "Be gone, Satan! For it is written, You shall worship the Lord your God and him only shall you serve" (Matt 4:9–10).

(*b*) But the hour is coming, and is now here, when the true worshipers will worship the Father in spirit and truth, for the Father is seeking such people to worship him (John 4:23).

(*c*) Go therefore and make disciples of all nations, baptizing them in the name of the Father and of the Son and of the Holy Spirit (Matt 28:19).

(*d*) Because they exchanged the truth about God for a lie and worshiped and served the creature rather than the Creator, who is blessed forever! Amen (Rom 1:25).

(*e*) Let no one disqualify you, insisting on asceticism and worship of angels, going on in detail about visions, puffed up without reason by his sensuous mind (Col 2:18).

(*f*) Then I fell down at his feet to worship him, but he said to me, "You must not do that! I am a fellow servant with you and your brothers who hold to the testimony of Jesus. Worship God." For the testimony of Jesus is the spirit of prophecy (Rev 19:10).

REMARKS: One of the controversies that divide Roman Catholics and Protestants is the relationship between worshipping God (called latria) and venerating Mary (called hyperdulia) and the saints (called dulia). Catholics insist they simply honor or pay devotion to Mary and the saints, while bestowing worship to God. Evangelicals point out that the Bible does not recognize a distinction between the terms dulia and latria in the context of religious worship, nor can a distinction be made lexicographically. Both terms trace back to the biblical usage of divine worship, and therefore no meaningful separation can be made between the two. We serve a jealous God who takes worship seriously—just as Uzzah realized the hard way when the Lord struck him dead (2 Sam 6:3–7).

QUESTION 22-3: HOW ARE WE TO OFFER OUR PRAYERS TO GOD?

ANSWER: Acceptable prayer is to be made in the name of the Son, *(a)* by the help of the Holy Spirit, *(b)* and according to his will. *(c)* It must be made with understanding, reverence, humility, fervency, faith, love, and perseverance. In like manner, corporate prayer must be made in a known language. *(d)*

(a) Whatever you ask in my name, this I will do, that the Father may be glorified in the Son. If you ask me anything in my name, I will do it (John 14:13–14).

(b) Likewise the Spirit helps us in our weakness. For we do not know what to pray for as we ought, but the Spirit himself intercedes for us with groanings too deep for words (Rom 8:26).

(c) And this is the confidence that we have toward him, that if we ask anything according to his will he hears us (1 John 5:14).

(d) Otherwise, if you give thanks with your spirit, how can anyone in the position of an outsider say "Amen to your thanksgiving when he does not know what you are saying? For you may be giving thanks well enough, but the other person is not being built up" (1 Cor 14:16–17).

REMARKS: It is remarkable to consider that the God of the universe listens to our prayers. In fact, the Bible teaches us that we should pray and also gives examples with respect to accomplishing this task. Perhaps the best known prayer is the Lord's Prayer. This brief communication with God serves as the Christian model as instructed by Christ. Included in this prayer are expressions of adoration and praise, confession of sins, thankfulness for God's goodness, petition for one's self and for others, and intercession.

QUESTION 22-4: WHAT SHALL WE PRAY FOR?

ANSWER: Prayer is to be made for things lawful and for all sorts of men living or that ever shall live. *(a) (b)*

(a) First of all, then, I urge that supplications, prayers, intercessions, and thanksgivings be made for all people, for kings and all who

are in high positions, that we may lead a peaceful and quiet life, godly and dignified in every way (1 Tim 2:1–2).

(b) "Now therefore may it please you to bless the house of your servant, so that it may continue forever before you. For you, O Lord GOD, have spoken, and with your blessing shall the house of your servant be blessed forever" (2 Sam 7:29).

REMARKS: It is worth noting here that the reason we pray for self and others is because the Lord uses our prayers to fulfill his divine plan. Some often wonder why Reformed Christians pray if God has ordained everything that shall come to pass. To this, the answer would be twofold: God commands us to pray, and God ordains the means as well as the ends to achieve his purpose.

QUESTION 22–5: WHAT PROHIBITIONS ARE ON PRAYER?

ANSWER: Prayer is not to be offered to the dead, *(a)* nor for those who have sinned the sin unto death. *(b)*

(a) Then his servants said to him, "What is this thing that you have done? You fasted and wept for the child while he was alive; but when the child died, you arose and ate food." He said, "While the child was still alive, I fasted and wept, for I said, 'Who knows whether the LORD will be gracious to me, that the child may live?' But now he is dead. Why should I fast? Can I bring him back again? I shall go to him, but he will not return to me" (2 Sam 12:21–23).

(b) If anyone sees his brother committing a sin not leading to death, he shall ask, and God will give him life—to those who commit sins that do not lead to death. There is sin that leads to death; I do not say that one should pray for that (1 John 5:16).

REMARKS: There is no biblical evidence that saints in heaven can hear our prayers. In fact, the idea of praying to the dead is more than abiblical, it is unbiblical. The Scripture condemns any attempt to contact the dead and declares it an abomination to the Lord (Deut 18:10–12; Isa 8:19, 19:3). On a practical level, there is no need to search for an intercessor in heaven since we have direct access to God through our mediator Jesus Christ (1 Tim 2:5). God hears all of our prayers, and he is the only one who can answer them so it is futile to seek assistance from anyone else.

QUESTION 22–6: WHAT ARE THE ASPECTS OF RELIGIOUS WORSHIP?

ANSWER: Reading the Scriptures, *(a)* preaching, and hearing the Word of God, *(b)* teaching and admonishing one another in psalms, hymns, and spiritual songs, singing with grace in our hearts to the Lord; *(c)* *(d)* as also the administration of baptism *(e)* and the Lord's Supper *(f)* are all aspects of religious worship.

(a) Until I come, devote yourself to the public reading of Scripture, to exhortation, to teaching (1 Tim 4:13).

(b) Preach the word; be ready in season and out of season; reprove, rebuke, and exhort, with complete patience and teaching (2 Tim 4:2).

(c) Let the word of Christ dwell in you richly, teaching and admonishing one another in all wisdom, singing psalms and hymns and spiritual songs, with thankfulness in your hearts to God (Col 3:16).

(d) Addressing one another in psalms and hymns and spiritual songs, singing and making melody to the Lord with your heart (Eph 5:19).

(e) "Go therefore and make disciples of all nations, baptizing them in the name of the Father and of the Son and of the Holy Spirit, teaching them to observe all that I have commanded you. And behold, I am with you always, to the end of the age" (Matt 28:19–20).

(f) For as often as you eat this bread and drink the cup, you proclaim the Lord's death until he comes (1 Cor 11:26).

REMARKS: Biblical worship is the natural response of the saved individual to give honor and praise to his Creator. The worship service is the time set aside each week to gather together with other believers to publicly acknowledge all the good gifts he has given, to praise him for what he is and what he has done, to learn about him more, and to obey his commands.

Question 22–7: Where and how often is God to be worshipped?

Answer: God is to be worshipped everywhere in spirit and in truth. *(a)* We are to worship the Lord in our homes daily *(b) (c)* and when alone, *(d)* in addition to public assemblies.

(a) I desire then that in every place the men should pray, lifting holy hands without anger or quarreling (1 Tim 2:8).

(b) A devout man who feared God with all his household, gave alms generously to the people, and prayed continually to God (Acts 10:2).

(c) Evening and morning and at noon I utter my complaint and moan, and he hears my voice (Ps 55:17).

(d) But when you pray, go into your room and shut the door and pray to your Father who is in secret. And your Father who sees in secret will reward you (Matt 6:6).

Remarks: God gave Israel four main features in the pattern for public worship that were to be observed. These include the Sabbath as a day of rest following six days of work; three annual feasts which included sacrifices; the Day of Atonement in which a scapegoat was sent into the wilderness as a sign of removing sins; and regular sacrifices through burnt offerings.

Question 22–8: What does the Christian Sabbath mean?

Answer: God appointed one day of the week for a sabbath to be kept holy unto him *(a)* which from the resurrection of Jesus Christ has been the first day of the week, known as the Lord's day. *(b) (c)*

(a) Remember the Sabbath day, to keep it holy (Ex 20:8).

(b) Now concerning the collection for the saints: as I directed the churches of Galatia, so you also are to do. On the first day of every week, each of you is to put something aside and store it up, as he may prosper, so that there will be no collecting when I come (1 Cor 16:1–2).

(c) On the first day of the week, when we were gathered together to break bread, Paul talked with them, intending to depart on the next day, and he prolonged his speech until midnight (Acts 20:7).

REMARKS: The Old Testament Sabbath was a memorial first observed in the Garden of Eden after creation. It eventually evolved into remembering God's deliverance of his people from Egyptian captivity. The New Testament church changed the Sabbath from the last day of the week to observing it on the first day as a way to celebrate Christ's death and resurrection. This symbolically points to a new creation and to the believer's redemption through the faithfulness of Jesus Christ.

QUESTION 22-9: HOW SHOULD CHRISTIANS KEEP THE SABBATH HOLY?

ANSWER: The Sabbath is kept holy to the Lord by preparing the heart for worship, by resting from normal worldly employment and recreations, *(a) (b)* and by giving oneself to public and private acts of worship for the whole time while carrying out duties of necessity and mercy. *(c)*

(a) "If you turn back your foot from the Sabbath, from doing your pleasure on my holy day, and call the Sabbath a delight and the holy day of the LORD honorable; if you honor it, not going your own ways, or seeking your own pleasure, or talking idly" (Isa 58:13).

(b) In those days I saw in Judah people treading winepresses on the Sabbath, and bringing in heaps of grain and loading them on donkeys, and also wine, grapes, figs, and all kinds of loads, which they brought into Jerusalem on the Sabbath day. And I warned them on the day when they sold food. Tyrians also, who lived in the city, brought in fish and all kinds of goods and sold them on the Sabbath to the people of Judah, in Jerusalem itself! Then I confronted the nobles of Judah and said to them, 'What is this evil thing that you are doing, profaning the Sabbath day? Did not your fathers act in this way, and did not our God bring all this disaster on us and on this city? Now you are bringing more wrath on Israel by profaning the Sabbath' (Neh 13:15–18).

(c) He went on from there and entered their synagogue. And a man was there with a withered hand. And they asked him, "Is it lawful to heal on the Sabbath?"—so that they might accuse him. He said to them, "Which one of you who has a sheep, if it falls into a pit on the Sabbath, will not take hold of it and lift it out? Of how much more value is a man than a sheep! So it is lawful to do good on the Sabbath." Then he said to the man, "Stretch out your hand." And the man stretched it out, and it was restored, healthy like the other (Matt 12:9–13).

REMARKS: Defining what exactly can and cannot take place on the Sabbath is not clearly set forth in Scripture. Those matters are best left between the individual and the Lord. Nevertheless, it is our duty as Christians to set aside all matters and give ourselves wholly to the worship of God for one day each week.

23

Oaths and Vows

QUESTION 23–1: WHAT IS A LAWFUL OATH?

ANSWER: A lawful oath is part of religious worship, wherein the person swearing in truth, righteousness, and judgement, sincerely calls upon God to witness what he swears, *(a) (b)* and to judge him according to its truthfulness. *(c) (d)*

(a) You shall not take the name of the LORD your God in vain, for the LORD will not hold him guiltless who takes his name in vain (Ex 20:7).

(b) You shall fear the LORD your God. You shall serve him and hold fast to him, and by his name you shall swear (Deut 10:20).

(c) If a man sins against his neighbor and is made to take an oath and comes and swears his oath before your altar in this house, then hear from heaven and act and judge your servants, repaying the guilty by bringing his conduct on his own head, and vindicating the righteous by rewarding him according to his righteousness (2 Chr 6:22–23).

(d) "And if you swear, 'As the LORD lives,' in truth, in justice, and in righteousness, then nations shall bless themselves in him, and in him shall they glory" (Jer 4:2).

REMARKS: The Anabaptists were a religious group who refused to take oaths as part of their rejection of the secular world. They pointed to Jesus' condemning of oaths in the Gospel of Matthew in which he commanded others to say simply "yes" or "no" (Matt 5:33–37). However, the historic interpretation of this passage is a condemnation of false or improper oaths used to deceive or manipulate others.

QUESTION 23-2: IS IT WRONG TO INVOKE THE NAME OF GOD WHEN TAKING AN OATH?

ANSWER: God is the only name by which men ought to swear; and it is to be used with all holy fear and reverence. The Bible prohibits swearing vainly or rashly, or by swearing at all by any other thing. *(a) (b) (c)* Yet, an oath is warranted by the Word of God to confirm truth and to end strife. *(d) (e)*

(a) But I say to you, Do not take an oath at all, either by heaven, for it is the throne of God (Matt 5:34).

(b) Let what you say be simply "Yes" or "No"; anything more than this comes from evil (Matt 5:37).

(c) But above all, my brothers, do not swear, either by heaven or by earth or by any other oath, but let your "yes" be yes and your "no" be no, so that you may not fall under condemnation (Jas 5:12).

(d) For people swear by something greater than themselves, and in all their disputes an oath is final for confirmation (Heb 6:16).

(e) But I call God to witness against me—it was to spare you that I refrained from coming again to Corinth (2 Cor 1:23).

REMARKS: It is a solemn affair when someone invokes God as a witness and should be treated with all seriousness. One must keep his commitment at all cost. Telling the truth demonstrates proper respect and dignity for our neighbors who are created in the image of God. Furthermore, honesty is essential to keeping and maintaining a healthy relationship with God and others. God's abhorrence for dishonesty is indicated by the ninth commandment (Ex 20:16).

QUESTION 23-3: ARE THERE ANY VOWS OR OATHS THAT A CHRISTIAN SHOULD NOT TAKE?

ANSWER: A vow is to be made to God alone and is to be made and performed with all religious care and faithfulness. *(a) (b)* Monastic vows of chastity, *(c) (d)* professed poverty, *(e)* and regular obedience, are so far from being degrees of higher perfection, that they are superstitious and sinful snares in which no Christian may entangle himself. *(f)*

(a) Make your vows to the LORD your God and perform them; let all around him bring gifts to him who is to be feared (Ps 76:11).

(b) Then Jacob made a vow, saying, "If God will be with me and will keep me in this way that I go, and will give me bread to eat and clothing to wear, so that I come again to my father's house in peace, then the LORD shall be my God, and this stone, which I have set up for a pillar, shall be God's house. And of all that you give me I will give a full tenth to you" (Gen 28:20–22).

(c) But because of the temptation to sexual immorality, each man should have his own wife and each woman her own husband (1 Cor 7:2).

(d) But if they cannot exercise self-control, they should marry. For it is better to marry than to burn with passion (1 Cor 7:9).

(e) Let the thief no longer steal, but rather let him labor, doing honest work with his own hands, so that he may have something to share with anyone in need (Eph 4:28).

(f) But he said to them, "Not everyone can receive this saying, but only those to whom it is given" (Matt 19:11).

REMARKS: The Gnostics were a heretical group that argued the material of the world was evil and promoted strict asceticism. They sought to teach abstinence from sexual relations within marriage and abstaining from eating certain foods. It is in this context that Paul condemned both ideas as "doctrines of demons" (1 Tim 4:3). However, Paul recognized certain benefits from remaining single by choice, but understood celibacy was not for everybody and corrected those who demanded vows of chastity.

24

Civil Government

QUESTION 24-1: WHAT IS THE ROLE OF CIVIL GOVERNMENT?

ANSWER: God has ordained civil government to be under him and over the people for his own glory and the public good. The Lord has armed rulers with the power of the sword for defense of the people and encouragement of others that do good and for the punishment of the wicked. *(a)*

  (a) Let every person be subject to the governing authorities. For there is no authority except from God, and those that exist have been instituted by God. Therefore whoever resists the authorities resists what God has appointed, and those who resist will incur judgment. For rulers are not a terror to good conduct, but to bad. Would you have no fear of the one who is in authority? Then do what is good, and you will receive his approval, for he is God's servant for your good. But if you do wrong, be afraid, for he does not bear the sword in vain. For he is the servant of God, an avenger who carries out God's wrath on the wrongdoer (Rom 13:1–4).

REMARKS: Some opponents of capital punishment make the argument that putting the guilty to death and holding to pro–life principles are inconsistent. They maintain that life should not be taken needlessly. Ironically, this is exactly why Christians support life at its most defenseless stage and uphold capital punishment for those who have committed egregious crimes against humanity. These principles are in perfect harmony with God's universal command given to Noah after the flood in which he outlined that any person who willfully took the life of another would be obligated to give up his own life as punishment for his sin (Gen 9:6).

QUESTION 24-2: IS IT PROPER FOR CHRISTIANS TO SERVE IN PUBLIC OFFICE?

ANSWER: It is lawful for Christians to accept and execute the office of a civil ruler when called, especially to maintain justice and peace. *(a) (b)*

(a) The God of Israel has spoken; the Rock of Israel has said to me: When one rules justly over men, ruling in the fear of God (2 Sam 23:3).

(b) "Give justice to the weak and the fatherless; maintain the right of the afflicted and the destitute. Rescue the weak and the needy; deliver them from the hand of the wicked" (Ps 82:3–4).

REMARKS: Civil government is the means by which God maintains order and discipline in communities and exists for the benefit of mankind. This is especially true when Christians hold positions of authority within government and adhere to biblical precepts. One Old Testament example is Joseph who saved the Egyptian people from starvation because of his favor with God (Gen 47:25). Had Joseph not been in a position of authority, the nation of Egypt would not have been spared the effects of the famine. In like manner, the role of the government requires making difficult moral and ethical decisions, which is undoubtedly best suited for the Christian to make.

QUESTION 24-3: HOW IS THE CHRISTIAN TO RESPOND TO THE CIVIL GOVERNMENT?

ANSWER: Since God sets up the civil government, we are to be subject in all lawful things commanded by them for conscience' sake. *(a) (b)* Furthermore, we ought to make supplications and prayers for all that are in authority, that under them we may live a quiet and peaceable life, in all godliness and honesty. *(c)*

(a) Therefore one must be in subjection, not only to avoid God's wrath but also for the sake of conscience. For because of this you also pay taxes, for the authorities are ministers of God, attending to this very thing. Pay to all what is owed to them: taxes to whom taxes are owed, revenue to whom revenue is owed, respect to whom respect is owed, honor to whom honor is owed (Rom 13:5–7).

(b) Honor everyone. Love the brotherhood. Fear God. Honor the emperor (1 Pet 2:17).

(c) First of all, then, I urge that supplications, prayers, intercessions, and thanksgivings be made for all people (1 Tim 2:1).

REMARKS: Christians are to submit to the government in all cases except when it forbids what God requires or requires what God forbids (Acts 4:18–31). Additionally, Christians have a duty to speak out on matters of morality on the basis of the Word of God. They are not to do so to incite violence but should work to persuade leaders to do what is pleasing to God.

25

Marriage

QUESTION 25–1: HOW DID GOD DESIGN MARRIAGE?

ANSWER: Marriage is to be between one man and one woman. Neither is it lawful for any man to have more than one wife, nor for any woman to have more than one husband at the same time. *(a) (b) (c)*

(a) Therefore a man shall leave his father and his mother and hold fast to his wife, and they shall become one flesh (Gen 2:24).

(b) Did he not make them one, with a portion of the Spirit in their union? And what was the one God seeking? Godly offspring. So guard yourselves in your spirit, and let none of you be faithless to the wife of your youth (Mal 2:15).

(c) And said, "Therefore a man shall leave his father and his mother and hold fast to his wife, and the two shall become one flesh? So they are no longer two but one flesh. What therefore God has joined together, let not man separate" (Matt 19:5–6).

REMARKS: Marriage is a covenant for life in which a man and a woman give themselves to each other on the promise to become one flesh (Gen 2:24). It is God's will that each are believers so that they can unite in the same faith and on the same principles. In order to understand what those are and the proper function of marriage, Paul draws a parallel to Christ's relationship with his church. This is to bring to light the significant role the husband has as leader and protector and the wife's responsibility to fulfill her role graciously (Eph 5:21–33). What many people misunderstand about the biblical relationship between husband and wife is not a matter of superiority and inferiority. Jesus was not inferior to the Father when he willingly submitted to the

Father's commands. Similarly, when a wife submits to her husband she is simply surrendering to God's ordained order.

QUESTION 25-2: WHAT IS THE PURPOSE OF MARRIAGE?

ANSWER: Marriage was ordained for the mutual help of husband and wife, *(a)* for the increase of mankind, *(b)* and for preventing sexual impurity. *(c) (d)*

 (a) And God blessed them. And God said to them, "Be fruitful and multiply and fill the earth and subdue it and have dominion over the fish of the sea and over the birds of the heavens and over every living thing that moves on the earth" (Gen 1:28).

 (b) Then the LORD God said, "It is not good that the man should be alone; I will make him a helper fit for him" (Gen 2:18).

 (c) But because of the temptation to sexual immorality, each man should have his own wife and each woman her own husband (1 Cor 7:2).

 (d) But if they cannot exercise self-control, they should marry. For it is better to marry than to burn with passion (1 Cor 7:9).

REMARKS: Marriage and the family are the oldest and most fundamental of all human institutions. The Bible presents the importance of spiritual guidance within the family and points to it as the training ground for a mature relationship with Christ. Parents have an obligation to their children to instruct them in righteousness (Deut 4:9; 6:6–9) and to discipline them as a means of corrective and loving training (Prov 1:8; 6:20; 13:24). A strong marriage will inevitably lead to a strong family whose main priority is to serve the Lord (Jos 24:15).

QUESTION 25-3: WHOM SHOULD A CHRISTIAN MARRY?

ANSWER: It is the duty of Christians to marry in the Lord. *(a)* Therefore, Christians are not to marry unbelievers and are not to be unequally yoked with those who profess another faith that leads to spiritual death. *(b)*

(a) A wife is bound to her husband as long as he lives. But if her husband dies, she is free to be married to whom she wishes, only in the Lord (1 Cor 7:39).

(b) And I confronted them and cursed them and beat some of them and pulled out their hair. And I made them take oath in the name of God, saying, "You shall not give your daughters to their sons, or take their daughters for your sons or for yourselves. Did not Solomon king of Israel sin on account of such women? Among the many nations there was no king like him, and he was beloved by his God, and God made him king over all Israel. Nevertheless, foreign women made even him to sin. Shall we then listen to you and do all this great evil and act treacherously against our God by marrying foreign women" (Neh 13:25–27)?

REMARKS: The New Testament recognizes that some believers are unequally yoked through later conversions in life. This issue was even addressed in Peter's epistle in which he wrote that wives were to be subject to their husbands even if those men were unbelievers (1 Pet 3:1). It was the ancient custom of Rome for the wife to adopt the religion of her husband, so Peter exhorted the Christian women to submit graciously to their husbands so that their gospel message would be presented in a good light through obedience.

26

The Church

QUESTION 26-1: WHAT IS MEANT BY THE TERM INVISIBLE CHURCH?

ANSWER: The invisible church consists of all of the elect that have been, are, or shall be gathered into one, under Christ, the head of church. *(a) (b) (c)*

(a) And to the assembly of the firstborn who are enrolled in heaven, and to God, the judge of all, and to the spirits of the righteous made perfect (Heb 12:23).

(b) And he is the head of the body, the church. He is the beginning, the firstborn from the dead, that in everything he might be pre-eminent (Col 1:18).

(c) As a plan for the fullness of time, to unite all things in him, things in heaven and things on earth (Eph 1:10).

REMARKS: When theologians speak of the invisible and visible church they are not making the claim that God has two separate churches. Jesus has only one bride. The two terms are used to describe the different aspects of the one church. The former deals with only those who are truly saved, while the latter refers to members who profess faith in Jesus. There is a great overlap between the two categories with every member of the invisible church belonging to the visible church but not every professing believer belonging to the invisible church.

QUESTION 26–2: WHAT IS MEANT BY THE TERM VISIBLE CHURCH?

ANSWER: The visible church refers to all persons throughout the world who profess the faith of the gospel and obedience unto God by Christ. *(a)*

   (a) To the church of God that is in Corinth, to those sanctified in Christ Jesus, called to be saints together with all those who in every place call upon the name of our Lord Jesus Christ, both their Lord and ours (1 Cor 1:2).

REMARKS: The Protestant Reformers were concerned with being able to recognize the marks of the true church. They turned to Scripture in order to accomplish this task and found at least two criteria: faithfully preaching the Word of God and administering the ordinances. Martin Luther—among other Christians—taught the keys of disciplines (Matt 16:19) were the third mark of a true church (Titus 1:13; 2:15; 3:10).

QUESTION 26–3: WILL CHURCHES EVER APOSTATIZE?

ANSWER: The purest churches are subject to mixture and error *(a)* and some have so perverted the gospel message that they are no longer churches of Christ. *(b) (c)* Nevertheless, Christ always has, and always will have churches made up of those who believe in him and make profession of his name. *(d)*

   (a) Read 1 Corinthians 5; Revelation 2 and 3

   (b) Fallen, fallen is Babylon the great! She has become a dwelling place for demons, a haunt for every unclean spirit, a haunt for every unclean bird, a haunt for every unclean and detestable beast (Rev 18:2).

   (c) Therefore God sends them a strong delusion, so that they may believe what is false, in order that all may be condemned who did not believe the truth but had pleasure in unrighteousness (2 Thess 2:11–12).

   (d) And I tell you, you are Peter, and on this rock I will build my church, and the gates of hell shall not prevail against it (Matt 16:18).

REMARKS: Many find comfort in believing that their church is the one true church that will remain free from corruption and error, but such thinking is self-delusional. When churches rely on tradition instead of the Word of God any doctrine or form of worship can be justified—especially if that church defines what tradition is. Churches who hold to this standard are caught in a vicious cycle of circular reasoning in which there can be no admitting error or room for reform. The only antidote for error or heresy is to subject every doctrine to the unchanging Word of God.

QUESTION 26–4: WHO IS THE HEAD OF THE CHURCH?

ANSWER: The Lord Jesus Christ is the head of the church in a supreme and sovereign manner. *(a) (b)*

(a) And he is the head of the body, the church. He is the beginning, the firstborn from the dead, that in everything he might be pre-eminent (Col 1:18).

(b) And he gave the apostles, the prophets, the evangelists, the shepherds and teachers, to equip the saints for the work of ministry, for building up the body of Christ (Eph 4:11–12).

REMARKS: The idea that the church needs a man who exercises supreme and universal primacy, both of honor and jurisdiction over the church of Christ is without biblical support. The church receives its guidance and growth from Jesus Christ, and it is energized by his power and ruled by the Word and the Holy Spirit. There can only be one head to any body and that one head is Jesus Christ our Lord.

QUESTION 26–5: IS CHURCH MEMBERSHIP IMPORTANT?

ANSWER: God commands those whom he called to salvation to walk together in particular churches for mutual edification and worship. *(a) (b)* Therefore, belonging to a local assembly is essential for gospel obedience.

(a) "If your brother sins against you, go and tell him his fault, between you and him alone. If he listens to you, you have gained your brother. But if he does not listen, take one or two others along with you, that every charge may be established by the evidence of two or three witnesses. If he refuses to listen to them, tell it to the church. And if he refuses to listen even to the church, let him be to you as a Gentile and a tax collector. Truly, I say to you, whatever you bind on earth shall be bound in heaven, and whatever you loose on earth shall be loosed in heaven. Again I say to you, if two of you agree on earth about anything they ask, it will be done for them by my Father in heaven. For where two or three are gathered in my name, there am I among them" (Matt 18:15–20).

(b) Not neglecting to meet together, as is habit of some, but encouraging one another, and all the more as you see the day drawing near (Heb 10:25).

REMARKS: One of the first indications of a lack of love for God and his neighbor is to refrain from joining in worship services with other Christians. The author of Hebrews warns the early Christians not to be like the Israelites who turned away from God (Heb 3:12). As fallen creatures, we need constant encouragement and daily exhortations unto righteousness so that we will not become hardened by the deceitfulness of sin (Heb 3:13).

QUESTION 26–6: WHAT OBLIGATIONS DO CHURCH MEMBERS HAVE TOWARDS EACH OTHER?

ANSWER: Church members must willingly walk together, giving themselves up to the Lord and to one another. (a)

(a) By their approval of this service, they will glorify God because of your submission flowing from your confession of the gospel of Christ, and the generosity of your contribution for them and for all others (2 Cor 9:13).

REMARKS: The only way Christians can grow into spiritual maturity is by obeying the command to assemble together in the Lord (Heb 10:25). The church provides several functions that Christians cannot obtain elsewhere including the faithful preaching of the Word, the administering of the ordinances, and public worship. Each is essential in order to have a healthy relationship with other believers and the Lord.

QUESTION 26-7: WHAT POWER HAS GOD GIVEN TO THE CHURCH?

ANSWER: God has declared in his Word that he has given power and authority to ensure proper worship and discipline. *(a) (b) (c) (d)*

(a) If he refuses to listen to them, tell it to the church. And if he refuses to listen even to the church, let him be to you as a Gentile and a tax collector. Truly, I say to you, whatever you bind on earth shall be bound in heaven, and whatever you loose on earth shall be loosed in heaven (Matt 18:17–18).

(b) When you are assembled in the name of the Lord Jesus and my spirit is present, with the power of our Lord Jesus, you are to deliver this man to Satan for the destruction of the flesh, so that his spirit may be saved in the day of the Lord (1 Cor 5:4–5).

(c) God judges those outside. "Purge the evil person from among you" (1 Cor 5:13).

(d) For such a one, this punishment by the majority is enough, so you should rather turn to forgive and comfort him, or he may be overwhelmed by excessive sorrow. So I beg you to reaffirm your love for him (2 Cor 2:6–8).

REMARKS: God gave power to the church to exercise discipline over Christians within its own fellowship. This serves as one primary reason why church membership is important in our spiritual lives. If we are under the care and instruction of a local church, then we will be held accountable to other Christians for our daily conduct. Church accountability is essential as a form of checks and balances to guide us through the course of our lives.

QUESTION 26-8: WHAT DOES CHRIST'S CHURCHES CONSIST OF?

ANSWER: Each local assembly consists of officers and members. The officers, known as elders and deacons, are to administer the ordinances and execute the power of duty entrusted to them. *(a) (b) (c)*

(a) Now from Miletus he sent to Ephesus and called the elders of the church to come to him (Acts 20:17).

(b) Pay careful attention to yourselves and to all the flock, in which the Holy Spirit has made you overseers, to care for the church of God, which he obtained with his own blood (Acts 20:28).

(c) Paul and Timothy, servants of Christ Jesus, To all the saints in Christ Jesus who are at Philippi, with the overseers and deacons (Phil 1:1).

REMARKS: The Old Testament required provision for the poor and needy (Ps 9:18), and the New Testament was no different. Greek speaking Christian widows were being neglected basic necessities so the twelve apostles instructed the church to choose seven men to attend to the needs of the widows so the apostles could devote themselves to the preaching of the Word. These chosen men were called deacons (Acts 6:1–6).

QUESTION 26–9: HOW ARE CHURCH LEADERS TO BE SET ASIDE FOR SPIRITUAL LEADERSHIP?

ANSWER: The church is to set aside qualified individuals by prayer and fasting followed by the laying on of hands. (a) (b) (c)

(a) And what they said pleased the whole gathering, and they chose Stephen, a man full of faith and of the Holy Spirit, and Philip, and Prochorus, and Nicanor, and Timon, and Parmenas, and Nicolaus, a proselyte of Antioch. These they set before the apostles, and they prayed and laid their hands on them (Acts 6:5–6).

(b) Do not neglect the gift you have, which was given you by prophecy when the council of elders laid their hands on you (1 Tim 4:14).

(c) And when they had appointed elders for them in every church, with prayer and fasting they committed them to the Lord in whom they had believed (Acts 14:23).

REMARKS: The Old Testament high priests used the Urim and Thummim to make important decisions for the Israelites (Ex 28:30). These were small stones used to determine God's will. Casting lots was a common practice used for important decisions including selecting Saul as king of Israel (1 Sam 10:20–21). The last reference to casting lots in Scripture is when Matthias was chosen to replace Judas (Acts

1:26). There is no evidence in the New Testament that God's people should cast lots to ascertain its church leaders, but should pray for God's will to be revealed.

QUESTION 26–10: WHAT PASTORAL DUTIES ARE TO BE PERFORMED, AND WHAT IS TO BE THE RELATIONSHIP OF A PASTOR WITH HIS PEOPLE?

ANSWER: It is the duty of the pastor to minister the Word of God and to pray all the while watching over the souls of those entrusted to his care since he must give an account to God. *(a) (b)* It is the duty of the people to give proper respect to the pastor and to support him financially so that he is not entangled in secular affairs. *(c)*

(a) But we will devote ourselves to prayer and to the ministry of the word (Acts 6:4).

(b) Obey your leaders and submit to them, for they are keeping watch over your souls, as those who will have to give an account. Let them do this with joy and not with groaning, for that would be of no advantage to you (Heb 13:17).

(c) Or is it only Barnabas and I who have no right to refrain from working for a living? Who serves as a soldier at his own expense? Who plants a vineyard without eating any of its fruit? Or who tends a flock without getting some of the milk? Do I say these things on human authority? Does not the Law say the same? For it is written in the Law of Moses, "You shall not muzzle an ox when it treads out the grain." Is it for oxen that God is concerned? Does he not speak entirely for our sake? It was written for our sake, because the plowman should plow in hope and the thresher thresh in hope of sharing in the crop. If we have sown spiritual things among you, is it too much if we reap material things from you? If others share this rightful claim on you, do not we even more (1 Cor 9:6–14)?

REMARKS: Elders are called to be overseers of God's people. The Lord gave to them special authority, so we are instructed to follow their lead (Heb 13:17). Paul tells us that anyone who seeks this position desires a noble task (1 Tim 3:1). He further provided a detailed list of who is qualified to take on this important position. The most notable are that elders have mature Christian lives and are well established in their personal affairs.

QUESTION 26-11: WHO MAY PREACH THE WORD?

ANSWER: The Word of God may be preached by anyone who is gifted and qualified by the Holy Spirit for the task and approved and called by the church. *(a)*

> *(a)* As each has received a gift, use it to serve one another, as good stewards of God's varied grace: whoever speaks, as one who speaks oracles of God; whoever serves, as one who serves by the strength that God supplies—in order that in everything God may be glorified through Jesus Christ. To him belong glory and dominion forever and ever. Amen (1 Pet 4:10–11).

REMARKS: The Bible notes the important role bishops and elders have in shepherding God's flock and provides an extensive list of requirements for the position. Paul listed as a requirement to be the husband of one wife directly after the qualification to be above reproach (1 Tim 3:2; Titus 1:6). This expression has been interpreted as a prohibition against polygamy, remarriage after divorce, or against marital infidelity. Most have understood this to be the latter given the widespread immorality in the Greco–Roman culture, but regardless as to how the phrase is interpreted, this expression alone should prove sufficient to dismiss the idea of ordaining anyone but men into the ministry.

27

Christian Fellowship

QUESTION 27-1: IN WHAT MANNER ARE ALL CHRISTIANS UNITED?

ANSWER: All Christians that are united to Jesus Christ, their head, by his Spirit, and faith, have fellowship in his graces, sufferings, death, resurrection, and glory. *(a) (b) (c) (d)*

(a) That which we have seen and heard we proclaim also to you, so that you too may have fellowship with us; and indeed our fellowship is with the Father and with his Son Jesus Christ (1 John 1:3).

(b) And from his fullness we have all received, grace upon grace (John 1:16).

(c) That I may know him and the power of his resurrection, and may share his sufferings, becoming like him in his death (Phil 3:10).

(d) For if we have been united with him in a death like his, we shall certainly be united with him in a resurrection like his. We know that our old self was crucified with him in order that the body of sin might be brought to nothing, so that we would no longer be enslaved to sin (Rom 6:5–6).

REMARKS: Antinomians were individuals who espoused the belief that Christians were under no obligation to keep the moral law. Instead, they emphasized grace and ignored personal responsibility. Paul emphatically rejected this doctrinal heresy. "What then? Are we to sin because we are not under the law but under grace? By no means" (Rom 6:15)! Paul went on to remind his readers that they were united with

Christ in his death, and with that union came the responsibility to put off sin for the glory of God.

QUESTION 27–2: WHAT OBLIGATIONS DO CHRISTIANS HAVE TOWARDS EACH OTHER?

ANSWER: Being united to one another in love, Christians have fellowship in each other's gifts and graces, *(a) (b) (c)* and are obliged to give to one another according to their needs and abilities to meet them. *(d) (e) (f) (g) (h) (i)*

(a) Rather, speaking the truth in love, we are to grow up in every way into him who is the head, into Christ, from whom the whole body, joined and held together by every joint with which it is equipped, when each part is working properly, makes the body grow so that it builds itself up in love (Eph 4:15–16).

(b) To each is given the manifestation of the Spirit for the common good (1 Cor 12:7).

(c) So let no one boast in men. For all things are yours, whether Paul or Apollos or Cephas or the world or life or death or the present or the future—all are yours, and you are Christ's, and Christ is God's (1 Cor 3:21–23).

(d) Therefore encourage one another and build one another up, just as you are doing (1 Thess 5:11).

(e) And we urge you, brothers, admonish the idle, encourage the fainthearted, help the weak, be patient with them all (1 Thess 5:14).

(f) That is, that we may be mutually encouraged by each other's faith, both yours and mine (Rom 1:12).

(g) But if anyone has the world's goods and sees his brother in need, yet closes his heart against him, how does God's love abide in him? Little children, let us not love in word or talk but in deed and in truth (1 John 3:17–18).

(h) So then, as we have opportunity, let us do good to everyone, and especially to those who are of the household of faith (Gal 6:10).

(i) So the disciples determined, everyone according to his ability, to send relief to the brothers living in Judea. And they did so, sending it to the elders by the hand of Barnabas and Saul (Acts 11:29–30).

REMARKS: The Christian journey consists of continual sacrifice. We are called to give to our brothers and sisters in Christ as each requires. No two individuals are alike, and each will require special attention for spiritual growth. When we devote ourselves to committing loving acts of kindness and forbearance, the desired result is the mutual edification of self and others.

QUESTION 27-3: WHAT SPIRITUAL RESPONSIBILITIES DO CHRISTIANS HAVE TOWARDS EACH OTHER?

ANSWER: Christians are bound to maintain a holy fellowship and communion in the worship of God and in performing such other spiritual services as tend to their mutual edification. *(a) (b)*

(a) And let us consider how to stir up one another to love and good works, not neglecting to meet together, as is the habit of some, but encouraging one another, and all the more as you see the Day drawing near (Heb 10:24–25).

(b) Take care, brothers, lest there be in any of you an evil, unbelieving heart, leading you to fall away from the living God. But exhort one another every day, as long as it is called "today," that none of you may be hardened by the deceitfulness of sin (Heb 3:12–13).

REMARKS: Believers are not given spiritual gifts for their own private benefit. They are to be used within the Christian community for the edification of others. It is a near impossible task for Christians to reach spiritual maturity if isolated from others and their gifts. Therefore, we are called to help others grow in grace and truth using the ability the Lord has given us.

28

Ordinances

Question 28-1: What is an ordinance?

Answer: An ordinance is a rite, appointed by the Lord Jesus, the only lawgiver, to be performed and continued in his church to the end of the world. *(a) (b)*

> *(a)* "Go therefore and make disciples of all nations, baptizing them in the name of the Father and of the Son and of the Holy Spirit, teaching them to observe all that I have commanded you. And behold, I am with you always, to the end of the age" (Matt 28:19–20).

> *(b)* For as often as you eat this bread and drink the cup, you proclaim the Lord's death until He comes (1 Cor 11:26).

Remarks: Scripture does not give us a technical name for the rites instituted by Christ. The Western Church uses the term sacraments, while the Eastern Orthodox Church, including various Protestant denominations, prefers mysteries or ordinances. Regardless of the term used, these rites are a sign and seal of a covenant relationship with God and are means of grace used to strengthen one's faith.

Question 28-2: What two ordinances did Jesus Christ institute?

Answer: Jesus Christ established baptism *(a)* and the Lord's supper *(b)* to be continued by the church until he returns.

> *(a)* "Go therefore and make disciples of all nations, baptizing them in the name of the Father and of the Son and of the Holy Spirit, teaching them to observe all that I have commanded you. And

behold, I am with you always, to the end of the age" (Matt 28:19–20).

(b) For as often as you eat this bread and drink the cup, you proclaim the Lord's death until He comes (1 Cor 11:26).

REMARKS: The medieval church included five additional rites as sacraments: confirmation, penance, marriage, ordination, and extreme unction. These five are not signs and seals of a covenant relationship with God and were never instituted by Christ.

QUESTION 28–3: WHO SHOULD ADMINISTER THE ORDINANCES?

ANSWER: Only those who are qualified and are called according to the commission of Christ are to administer ordinances. *(a) (b)*

(a) "Go therefore and make disciples of all the nations, baptizing them in the name of the Father and the Son and the Holy Spirit" (Matt 28:19).

(b) This is how one should regard us, as servants of Christ and stewards of the mysteries of God (1 Cor 4:1).

REMARKS: One of the ideas presented in the letter to Timothy is the character of the man who is to be an elder or overseer. Paul indicates in his epistle that he is to be "above reproach" (1 Tim 3:2). This expression does not mean that an elder is to be without sin. Rather, it simply indicates the elder is to be in good standing with non-Christians so that he does not fall into disgrace (1 Tim 3:7).

29

Baptism

QUESTION 29-1: WHAT DOES BAPTISM SIGNIFY?

ANSWER: Baptism is a sign of fellowship with Jesus Christ in his death and resurrection; of being engrafted into him; *(a) (b) (c)* of remission of sins; *(d) (e)* and of his giving up unto God, through Jesus Christ, to live and to walk in newness of life. *(f)*

> *(a)* Do you not know that all of us who have been baptized into Christ Jesus were baptized into his death? We were buried therefore with him by baptism into death, in order that, just as Christ was raised from the dead by the glory of the Father, we too might walk in newness of life. For if we have been united with him in a death like his, we shall certainly be united with him in a resurrection like his (Rom 6:3–5).

> *(b)* Having been buried with him in baptism, in which you were also raised with him through faith in the powerful working of God, who raised him from the dead (Col 2:12).

> *(c)* For as many of you as were baptized into Christ have put on Christ (Gal 3:27).

> *(d)* John appeared, baptizing in the wilderness and proclaiming a baptism of repentance for the forgiveness of sins (Mark 1:4).

> *(e)* And now why do you wait? Rise and be baptized and wash away your sins, calling on his name (Acts 22:16).

> *(f)* We were buried therefore with him by baptism into death, in order that, just as Christ was raised from the dead by the glory of the Father, we too might walk in newness of life (Rom 6:4).

REMARKS: Christian baptism signifies cleansing. It is a sign from God that believers have had their sins washed away with the blood of Jesus, and that the Holy Spirit has brought regeneration and new life. Baptism is also a sign and seal that all true believers are kept safe in Christ forever and that he will lose none (John 10:28).

QUESTION 29–2: WHO SHOULD BE ALLOWED TO PARTICIPATE IN BAPTISM?

ANSWER: Those who profess repentance towards God, faith in, and obedience to our Lord Jesus, are the only proper subjects of this ordinance. *(a) (b) (c) (d) (e)*

(a) Whoever believes and is baptized will be saved, but whoever does not believe will be condemned (Mark 16:16).

(b) And as they were going along the road they came to some water, and the eunuch said, "See, here is water! What prevents me from being baptized?" And Philip said, "If you believe with all your heart, you may." And he replied, "I believe that Jesus Christ is the Son of God" (Acts 8:36–37).

(c) So those who received his word were baptized, and there were added that day about three thousand souls (Acts 2:41).

(d) But when they believed Philip as he preached good news about the kingdom of God and the name of Jesus Christ, they were baptized, both men and women (Acts 8:12).

(e) Crispus, the ruler of the synagogue, believed in the Lord, together with his entire household. And many of the Corinthians hearing Paul believed and were baptized (Acts 18:8).

REMARKS: The scriptural case for baptizing infants rests largely on the parallel between the Old Testament circumcision and the New Testament baptism as signs and seals of a covenant with God. Further support for paedobaptism resides with the claim that entire New Testament households were baptized—presumably to include infants. The Baptist would respond that circumcision was primarily a sign of Jewish ethnicity and limited only to male infants. Moreover, under the new covenant faith is required before baptism. And finally, one cannot state positively but can only assume that infants were among those baptized in New Testament households. The totality of scriptural passages concerning baptism reveals a biblical paradigm in which we find that a confession of faith served as a requirement before the believer was baptized.

QUESTION 29–3: WHAT IS THE PROPER BAPTISMAL FORMULA?

ANSWER: The professing believer is to be baptized in water in the name of the Father, Son, and Holy Spirit. *(a)*

(a) "Go therefore and make disciples of all nations, baptizing them in the name of the Father and of the Son and of the Holy Spirit" (Matt 28:19).

REMARKS: Christ's final appearance to his apostles included the command to baptize believers in the name of the Father, the Son, and the Holy Spirit (Matt 28:19). Believers are baptized in the three Persons of the Godhead as a sign that they are under the control and direction of the triune God.

QUESTION 29–4: WHAT IS THE PROPER MODE OF BAPTISM?

ANSWER: Immersion or dipping of the person in water is necessary to the due administration of this ordinance. *(a) (b)*

(a) And when Jesus was baptized, immediately he went up from the water, and behold, the heavens were opened to him, and he saw the Spirit of God descending like a dove and coming to rest on him (Matt 3:16).

(b) John also was baptizing at Aenon near Salim, because water was plentiful there, and people were coming and being baptized (John 3:23).

REMARKS: There is not a general consensus among Baptists concerning the proper mode of baptism. Some believe full immersion is biblically mandated, while others are satisfied with dipping or sprinkling, but all three modes satisfy the Greek verb baptizo. The importance of baptism is not the prescribed method but the symbolism of being cleansed.

30

The Lord's Supper

QUESTION 30-1: WHY DID CHRIST INSTITUTE THE LORD'S SUPPER?

ANSWER: Christ instituted the Lord's Supper for the continual remembrance of the sacrifice in his death, *(a)* for spiritual nourishment and growth in him, for the believer's commitment to all gospel duties, and to be a bond and pledge of communion with Christ and with each other. *(b) (c)*

(a) For I received from the Lord what I also delivered to you, that the Lord Jesus on the night when he was betrayed took bread, and when he had given thanks, he broke it, and said, "This is my body which is for you. Do this in remembrance of me." In the same way also he took the cup, after supper, saying, "This cup is the new covenant in my blood. Do this, as often as you drink it, in remembrance of me." For as often as you eat this bread and drink the cup, you proclaim the Lord's death until he comes (1 Cor 11:23–26).

(b) The cup of blessing that we bless, is it not a participation in the blood of Christ? The bread that we break, is it not a participation in the body of Christ? Because there is one bread, we who are many are one body, for we all partake of the one bread (1 Cor 10:16–17).

(c) You cannot drink the cup of the Lord and the cup of demons. You cannot partake of the table of the Lord and the table of demons (1 Cor 10:21).

REMARKS: The Lord's Supper has an additional meaning for Christians. It has particular importance in that it points towards a great moment that is yet to come. The Lord promised his disciples that he would come again. When we partake in the Lord's Supper we remember his pledge to return for all who believe (Heb 9:28).

QUESTION 30–2: IS JESUS CHRIST SACRIFICED AGAIN DURING THE LORD'S SUPPER?

ANSWER: Christ is not offered up to his Father, nor any real sacrifice made at all for the remission of sin of the living or dead, but only as a memorial of that one offering up of himself by himself upon the cross, once for all. *(a) (b)*

(a) Nor was it to offer himself repeatedly, as the high priest enters the holy places every year with blood not his own, for then he would have had to suffer repeatedly since the foundation of the world. But as it is, he has appeared once for all at the end of the ages to put away sin by the sacrifice of himself (Heb 9:25–26).

(b) So Christ, having been offered once to bear the sins of many, will appear a second time, not to deal with sin but to save those who are eagerly waiting for him (Heb 9:28).

REMARKS: The Fourth Lateran Council officially declared in AD 1215 that Christ is present in the elements by transubstantiation. What this means is that the bread and wine are miraculously transformed into the body and blood of Christ, even though the elements retain their form. The Protestant Reformers insisted that transubstantiation repeated the sacrifice of Jesus on the cross and that it denied the sufficiency of the atonement.

QUESTION 30–3: HOW IS THE LORD'S SUPPER TO BE ADMINISTERED?

ANSWER: The Lord Jesus appointed his ministers to pray and to bless the elements of bread and wine, thereby setting them apart for a holy use. *(a)*

(a) For I received from the Lord what I also delivered to you, that the Lord Jesus on the night when he was betrayed took bread,

and when he had given thanks, he broke it, and said, "This is my body which is for you. Do this in remembrance of me." In the same way also he took the cup, after supper, saying, "This cup is the new covenant in my blood. Do this, as often as you drink it, in remembrance of me." For as often as you eat this bread and drink the cup, you proclaim the Lord's death until he comes (1 Cor 11:23–26).

REMARKS: The regularity with which the Lord's Supper is observed is at the discretion of local assemblies. Some churches partake weekly while others offer on a less frequent basis. The biblical example of New Testament churches shows the Lord's Supper being observed weekly (Acts 20:7) and for good reason. Just as our bodies need daily nourishment, our spiritual diets are in need of constant replenishment.

QUESTION 30–4: HOW IS CHRIST REMEMBERED AND RECEIVED THROUGH OBSERVANCE OF THE LORD'S SUPPER?

ANSWER: Worthy receivers, outwardly partaking of the visible elements in this ordinance, spiritually receive and feed upon Christ crucified and all the benefits of his death. *(a) (b)*

> *(a)* The cup of blessing that we bless, is it not a participation in the blood of Christ? The bread that we break, is it not a participation in the body of Christ (1 Cor 10:16)?

> *(b)* For I received from the Lord what I also delivered to you, that the Lord Jesus on the night when he was betrayed took bread, and when he had given thanks, he broke it, and said, "This is my body which is for you. Do this in remembrance of me." In the same way also he took the cup, after supper, saying, "This cup is the new covenant in my blood. Do this, as often as you drink it, in remembrance of me." For as often as you eat this bread and drink the cup, you proclaim the Lord's death until he comes (1 Cor 11:23–26).

REMARKS: The Protestant Reformers rejected the Catholic doctrine of transubstantiation, but they could not come to an agreement on what form Christ was present—if any. Martin Luther's doctrine of consubstantiation was the closest to transubstantiation in that he insisted Christ's body and blood are present in, with, and under the elements. The Swiss Reformer Ulrich Zwingli believed the Lord's Supper was symbolic only. He denied Christ was present, insisting that the risen Savior was in heaven. John Calvin taught the Holy Spirit raises the believer in faith to be with the Christ, though in an indescribable manner.

QUESTION 30–5: SHOULD ANYONE REFRAIN FROM PARTICIPATING IN THE LORD'S SUPPER?

ANSWER: All unbelievers, who are unfit to enjoy communion with Christ, are unworthy of the Lord's table and cannot participate without sinning against God. *(a)* Yet, whoever receives the elements unworthily is guilty of the body and blood of the Lord, eating and drinking judgment to himself. *(b) (c)*

(a) Do not be unequally yoked with unbelievers. For what partnership has righteousness with lawlessness? Or what fellowship has light with darkness? What accord has Christ with Belial? Or what portion does a believer share with an unbeliever (2 Cor 6:14–15)?

(b) For anyone who eats and drinks without discerning the body eats and drinks judgment on himself (1 Cor 11:29).

(c) Do not give dogs what is holy, and do not throw your pearls before pigs, lest they trample them underfoot and turn to attack you (Matt 7:6).

REMARKS: Paul's counsel to the Corinthians was to conduct self–examination before coming to the Lord's table. This did not mean that sinners were not aloud to participate, but it was a warning that each individual must come to the Lord's Supper with a sincere love for Christ and others and with confessed sins. The consequence of eating and drinking unworthily can bring God's judgement upon those who neglect serious inward reflection (1 Cor 11:28–29).

31

Death and the Resurrection

QUESTION 31-1: WHERE DOES THE SOUL GO AFTER DEATH?

ANSWER: The souls of the righteous are made perfect in holiness and are received into paradise where they are with Christ, and behold the face of God in light and glory, waiting for the full redemption of their bodies. *(a) (b) (c) (d)* The unrighteous are cast into hell to face eternal torment and utter darkness until the judgment of the great day. *(e) (f)*

(a) And he said to him, "Truly, I say to you, today you will be with me in Paradise" (Luke 23:43).

(b) So we are always of good courage. We know that while we are at home in the body we are away from the Lord, for we walk by faith, not by sight. Yes, we are of good courage, and we would rather be away from the body and at home with the Lord (2 Cor 5:6–8).

(c) I am hard pressed between the two. My desire is to depart and be with Christ, for that is far better (Phil 1:23).

(d) And to the assembly of the firstborn who are enrolled in heaven, and to God, the judge of all, and to the spirits of the righteous made perfect (Heb 12:23).

(e) And the angels who did not stay within their own position of authority, but left their proper dwelling, he has kept in eternal chains under gloomy darkness until the judgment of the great day—just as Sodom and Gomorrah and the surrounding cities, which likewise indulged in sexual immorality and pursued un-natural desire, serve as an example by undergoing a punishment of eternal fire (Jude 1:6–7).

(f) And in Hades, being in torment, he lifted up his eyes and saw Abraham far off and Lazarus at his side. And he called out, "Father Abraham, have mercy on me, and send Lazarus to dip the end of his finger in water and cool my tongue, for I am in anguish in this flame" (Luke 16:23–24).

REMARKS: Those who do not believe that the souls of believers are made perfect in holiness and enter into heaven teach that there is a purgatorial discipline for sins. It is in purgatory that temporal sins are atoned for in a purifying fire by the suffering of atonement known as satispassio. But those who do not believe in purgatory point out that Paul and the thief on the cross expected to be in heaven with Christ immediately after death. Furthermore, many insist that when we stand before God we do so clothed in the righteousness of Christ and not in our own goodness or righteousness, worked out through our own sufferings in purgatory. Such a doctrine misunderstands the biblical view of justification and what it means to be in purified in Christ.

QUESTION 31–2: WHAT WILL HAPPEN TO THE CHRISTIANS AT THE SECOND COMING?

ANSWER: At the last day, the saints that are found alive shall not sleep but will be changed; *(a) (b)* and all the dead shall be raised up with the same bodies and none other. *(c)*

(a) Behold! I tell you a mystery. We shall not all sleep, but we shall all be changed, in a moment, in the twinkling of an eye, at the last trumpet. For the trumpet will sound, and the dead will be raised imperishable, and we shall be changed (1 Cor 15:51–52).

(b) Then we who are alive, who are left, will be caught up together with them in the clouds to meet the Lord in the air, and so we will always be with the Lord (1 Thess 4:17).

(c) And after my skin has been thus destroyed, yet in my flesh I shall see God, whom I shall see for myself, and my eyes shall behold, and not another. My heart faints within me (Job 19:26–27)!

REMARKS: We are told that Christ's coming will be a spectacular event in which he will descend from the clouds, heralded by a trumpet, a shout, and the voice of an archangel (1 Thess 4:16–17). Those who have died in Christ and those who are still living will be caught up in the air to meet the Lord and will be with him forever. Some, however, have championed the idea that Christians will be taken out of this world for a period of time after which Christ will appear a third time to complete his Second Coming. But this idea first introduced in the nineteenth century lacks scriptural foundation. No one but the Father knows the day or hour in which the Lord will return, but we know that he will come a second time for all who believe (Heb 9:28).

QUESTION 31–3: WHAT WILL HAPPEN TO THE UNRIGHTEOUS AT THE SECOND COMING?

ANSWER: The unrighteous shall be raised by the power of Christ to dishonor, while the bodies of the just will be raised to honor and will be made conformable to his own glorious body. *(a) (b) (c)*

(a) Having a hope in God, which these men themselves accept, that there will be a resurrection of both the just and the unjust (Acts 24:15).

(b) Do not marvel at this, for an hour is coming when all who are in the tombs will hear his voice and come out, those who have done good to the resurrection of life, and those who have done evil to the resurrection of judgment (John 5:28–29).

(c) Who will transform our lowly body to be like his glorious body, by the power that enables him even to subject all things to himself (Phil 3:21).

REMARKS: The biblical picture of hell is a place of eternal punishment. It is described as a lake of fire (Jude 1:7) and utter darkness, (v.13) in which there is weeping and gnashing of teeth (Matt 8:12). Some have suggested that these images are symbolic only. Be that as it may, the important thing to remember is that hell is a place of eternal torment and should instill terror in every one of us. The graphic portrayal of hell is designed to teach us about the real consequences of our sins and to direct us to the grace of God that will save us from such a place. God warns us because he is merciful and does not delight in the death of the wicked (Ezek 33:11).

32

The Last Judgement

QUESTION 32–1: WHAT WILL HAPPEN AT THE LAST JUDGEMENT?

ANSWER: God has appointed a day wherein he will judge the world in righteousness by Jesus Christ *(a) (b)* to whom all power and judgement are given by the Father. In that day, the fallen angels will be judged *(c)* *(d)* and all persons that have lived upon the earth shall appear before the tribunal of Christ to give account of their thoughts, words, and deeds. Everyone shall receive according to what has been done in the body, whether good or evil. *(e) (f) (g)*

(a) Because he has fixed a day on which he will judge the world in righteousness by a man whom he has appointed; and of this he has given assurance to all by raising him from the dead (Acts 17:31).

(b) The Father judges no one, but has given all judgment to the Son (John 5:22).

(c) Do you not know that we are to judge angels? How much more, then, matters pertaining to this life (1 Cor 6:3)!

(d) And the angels who did not stay within their own position of authority, but left their proper dwelling, he has kept in eternal chains under gloomy darkness until the judgment of the great day— (Jude 1:6).

(e) For we must all appear before the judgment seat of Christ, so that each one may receive what is due for what he has done in the body, whether good or evil (2 Cor 5:10).

(f) For God will bring every deed into judgment, with every secret thing, whether good or evil (Eccl 12:14).

(g) I tell you, on the day of judgment people will give account for every careless word they speak (Matt 12:36).

REMARKS: The entire human race will be brought up at the Second Coming. Some will be raised for the "second death" for their sins, while the rest will undergo an immediate transformation (1 Cor 15:50–54). The resurrection bodies will be like Christ's with respect to being eternal, imperishable, and capable of entering heaven. Christians will also be able to recognize one another, just as the disciples were able to recognize their risen Savior.

QUESTION 32–2: WHY IS THERE A FINAL JUDGEMENT?

ANSWER: The final judgement is appointed for the displaying of the glory of God's mercy in the eternal salvation of the elect and of his justice in the eternal damnation of the wicked and disobedient. *(a)*

(a) What if God, desiring to show his wrath and to make known his power, has endured with much patience vessels of wrath prepared for destruction, in order to make known the riches of his glory for vessels of mercy, which he has prepared beforehand for glory (Rom 9:22–23).

REMARKS: It is a difficult concept for people to think of a good God who punishes sinners, but the reality is that God cannot tolerate sin in any form. His holiness will not allow it. God's purity will not permit him to turn away from sin. Instead, his hatred towards sin results in the just judgements that are rewarded to the wicked which are glorious and praiseworthy. We can also take comfort in knowing that God's absolute holiness assures that God's treatment of sinners will always be perfect and just.

QUESTION 32–3: WHAT WILL HAPPEN TO THOSE THAT JESUS CHRIST DEEMS RIGHTEOUS?

ANSWER: The righteous will receive eternal life and an everlasting reward in the presence of the Lord. *(a) (b) (c)*

(a) His master said to him, "Well done, good and faithful servant. You have been faithful over a little; I will set you over much. Enter into the joy of your master" (Matt 25:21).

(b) Then the King will say to those on his right, "Come, you who are blessed by my Father, inherit the kingdom prepared for you from the foundation of the world" (Matt 25:34).

(c) Henceforth there is laid up for me the crown of righteousness, which the Lord, the righteous judge, will award to me on that Day, and not only to me but also to all who have loved his appearing (2 Tim 4:8).

REMARKS: Heaven is the biblical term for the dwelling place of God. It is there that Christians have the promise of eternally residing with Christ in a place of rest (John 14:2), where there is no sorrow, pain, or death (Rev 21:4). Heaven will be a joyous place where we are able to fulfill our chief purpose for being created: to glorify God and to enjoy him forever.

QUESTION 32–4: WHAT WILL HAPPEN TO THOSE THAT JESUS CHRIST CONDEMNS?

ANSWER: The wicked that do not know God will be cast into everlasting torment *(a) (b)* where they will be separated eternally from God. *(c)*

(a) And these will go away into eternal punishment, but the righteous into eternal life (Matt 25:46).

(b) Where their worm does not die and the fire is not quenched (Mark 9:48).

(c) And to grant relief to you who are afflicted as well as to us, when the Lord Jesus is revealed from heaven with his mighty angels in flaming fire, inflicting vengeance on those who do not know God and on those who do not obey the gospel of our Lord Jesus. They will suffer the punishment of eternal destruction, away from the presence of the Lord and from the glory of his might, when he comes on that day to be glorified in his saints, and to be marveled at among all who have believed, because our testimony to you was believed (2 Thess 1:7–10).

REMARKS: The Bible describes hell as a place of eternal "weeping and gnashing of teeth." This graphic picture is to help us confront the horrific reality of what is to come for anyone who loves sin more than God. The sobering reality is that everyone will eventually recognize there is only one Lord. The difference is that those who do so in this life will be spared eternal damnation, while those who reject God now will only realize their mistake after it is too late. Nevertheless, those who are condemned will know that they willingly chose to follow their own desires rather than to obey God and his Word.

QUESTION 32–5: WHAT IS THE ATTITUDE OF THE RIGHTEOUS COMPARED TO THAT OF THE UNRIGHTEOUS WITH RESPECT TO THE LAST JUDGEMENT?

ANSWER: The righteous are persuaded that there shall be a day of judgment, both to deter all men from sin, *(a)* and for the greater consolation of the godly in their temporal trials. *(b)* In contrast, the unrighteous embrace a false security and fail to watch for the Lord's return, *(c) (d)* and are not prepared to say: Come Lord Jesus, come quickly. *(e)* Amen.

(a) For we must all appear before the judgment seat of Christ, so that each one may receive what is due for what he has done in the body, whether good or evil. Therefore, knowing the fear of the Lord, we persuade others. But what we are is known to God, and I hope it is known also to your conscience (2 Cor 5:10–11).

(b) This is evidence of the righteous judgment of God, that you may be considered worthy of the kingdom of God, for which you are also suffering—since indeed God considers it just to repay with affliction those who afflict you, and to grant relief to you who are afflicted as well as to us, when the Lord Jesus is revealed from heaven with his mighty angels (2 Thess 1:5–7).

(c) Therefore stay awake—for you do not know when the master of the house will come, in the evening, or at midnight, or when the rooster crows, or in the morning—lest he come suddenly and find you asleep. And what I say to you I say to all: Stay awake (Mark 13:35–37).

(d) "Stay dressed for action and keep your lamps burning, and be like men who are waiting for their master to come home from the wedding feast, so that they may open the door to him at once when he comes and knocks. Blessed are those servants whom the master finds awake when he comes. Truly, I say to you, he

will dress himself for service and have them recline at table, and he will come and serve them. If he comes in the second watch, or in the third, and finds them awake, blessed are those servants! But know this, that if the master of the house had known at what hour the thief was coming, he would not have left his house to be broken into. You also must be ready, for the Son of Man is coming at an hour you do not expect" (Luke 12:35–40).

(e) He who testifies to these things says, "Surely I am coming soon." Amen. Come, Lord Jesus (Rev 22:20)!

REMARKS: The Christian attitude towards the end should be one of longing for Jesus to return. Our thoughts and prayers should constantly be for the realization of the Second Coming. We should live our lives as if it were the last day and should always be prepared for the return of Christ. This biblical attitude towards our present situation will help us overcome our struggles and will give us hope for today.

Bibliography

Bridges, Jerry. *The Pursuit of Holiness*. 3d ed. Colorado Springs, CO: NavPress, 2006.

Church, Leslie. *Matthew Henry's Commentary*. 13th ed. Grand Rapids, MI: Zondervan, 1961.

Godfrey, Robert, et al. *Sola Scriptura: The Protestant Position on the Bible*. Morgan, PA: Soli Deo Gloria, 1995.

Jeffrey, Peter. *Bitesize Theology: An ABC of the Christian Faith*. 6th ed. Darlington, EN: Evangelical, 2007.

Hendriksen, William. *New Testament Commentary*. 10th ed. Grand Rapids, MI: Baker Book House, 2002.

Kimbro, Reginald. *The Gospel According to Dispensationalism: A doctrinal survey of the system that permeated Fundamentalism*. Toronto, ON: Wittenburg, 1995.

Kistemaker, Simon. *New Testament Commentary*. 4th ed. Grand Rapids, MI: Baker Book House, 2002.

Murrell, Adam. *Predestined to Believe: Common Objections to the Reformed Faith Answered*. Eugene, OR: Resource, 2007.

Sproul, R. C. *The Reformation Study Bible*. Lake Mary, FL: Ligonier, 2005.

Svendsen, Eric. *Evangelical Answers: A Critique of Current Roman Catholic Apologists*. Lindenhurst, NY: Reformation, 1999.

Webster, William. *The Gospel of the Reformation: Salvation From the Guilt of Power of Sin*. Battle Ground, WA: Christian Resources, 1997.

White, James. *The Forgotten Trinity: Recovering the Heart of Christian Belief*. Minneapolis, MN: Bethany House, 1998.

———. *The Roman Catholic Controversy: Catholics and Protestants—Do the Differences Still Matter?* Minneapolis, MN: Bethany House, 1996.

www.ingramcontent.com/pod-product-compliance
Lightning Source LLC
Chambersburg PA
CBHW060312100426
42812CB00003B/752